Praise for *On the Move*

"This new edition of *On the Move* comes as a most timely contribution to the topic of the Latino presence in the United States. Moises Sandoval's historical account of the church and Latinos in the United States has for years been a primary source for those who either serve or are preparing to serve in pastoral settings. This new edition adds important data which enriches this fascinating account. Its concise presentation makes it readable and affordable."

—MOST REV. RICARDO RAMIREZ, CSB,
DIOCESE OF LAS CRUCES, NEW MEXICO

"In broad strokes and with deep understanding, Moises Sandoval skillfully provides us with a clear picture of the 'History of the Hispanic Church in the United States.' For more than the past three decades, he has not only been a witness to and reporter of that history, but also a participant. This has given him a perspective resulting in passionate solidarity with those about whom he writes."

—REV. JUAN ROMERO,
OUR LADY OF GUADALUPE CHURCH,
PALM SPRINGS, CALIFORNIA

"Thank God that Moises Sandoval has updated his now classic popular history of the US Hispanic church. In a concise and highly accessible way Sandoval portrays the ongoing drama of that faith community with competence and verve. Demographics is destiny. As that one-time Hispanic undercurrent becomes the main flow of US Catholicism and Protestantism this work can only gain importance and relevance."

—*Allan Figueroa Deck, SJ,*
President,
Loyola Institute for Spirituality

"Sandoval's book is a real gem! Reads like a diary! Such a book could have only been written by someone who has lived most of the journey himself and has reflected critically on the tears and laughter, the persistence and perseverance, the sacrifices and the fiestas of a people determined to remain faithful Catholics. It is truly a must for anyone wanting to understand the pilgrimage of faith of the Hispanic peoples in the USA."

—*Rev. Virgilio Elizondo,*
Mexican American Cultural Center,
San Antonio, Texas

On the Move remains the only compact yet comprehensive history of Hispanic Christianity in the United States. Sandoval excels in providing the larger social context. Strongly committed to his people and his faith, he argues that most of the church has continuously failed to respond adequately to the changing Hispanic reality. The theme of a great lack of sufficient numbers of Hispanic church leaders runs throughout the history. While bringing this account up to date, this revised edition includes new sections on the indigenous contributions to Hispanic religiosity, the factors aiding the Spanish conquest, and completely rewritten introductory and concluding assessments."

—*Rev. Robert E. Wright, OMI,*
National Coordinator,
CEHILA USA

ON THE MOVE

A History of the Hispanic Church in the United States

Moises Sandoval

ORBIS BOOKS

Maryknoll, New York 10545

Founded in 1970, Orbis Books endeavors to publish works that enlighten the mind, nourish the spirit, and challenge the conscience. The publishing arm of the Maryknoll Fathers and Brothers, Orbis seeks to explore the global dimensions of the Christian faith and mission, to invite dialogue with diverse cultures and religious traditions, and to serve the cause of reconciliation and peace. The books published reflect the views of their authors and do not represent the official position of the Maryknoll Society. To learn more about Maryknoll and Orbis Books, please visit our website at www.maryknoll.org.

Library of Congress Cataloging-in-Publication Data

Sandoval, Moises.
    On the move : a history of the Hispanic church in the United States / Moises Sandoval. — 2nd rev. ed.
        p. cm.
    Includes bibliographical references and index.
    ISBN-13: 978–1–57075–676–4 (pbk.)
    1. Hispanic Americans—Religion. 2. Hispanic American Catholics—History. 3. United States—Church history. I. Title.
    BR563.H57S26 2006
    277.3'008968—dc22

                                                    2006009744

Contents

Part I
Contributions of Pre-Columbian Religion

Part II
Conquest and Evangelization by the Spaniards

Part III
American Conquest and the Melting-Pot Church

Part IV
The Church of the Poor Comes of Age

Foreword

The decision to publish a second edition of Moises Sandoval's *On the Move* is a clear indication of the book's value. This second edition contains a rich and intricate treatment of the indigenous roots of Hispanic Christianity. This new section explains how the "seeds of the word" were embedded in the indigenous cultures long before European Christianity arrived. The Indian peoples of the Americas already had limited notions of such Christian concepts as death and resurrection, redeeming sacrifice, union with the divine through sacred meals, and the incarnation of the deity. It is obvious that Moises Sandoval has amply researched pre-Columbian history and anthropology. The data he provides covers the Western hemisphere, and the analysis he offers is insightful and enlightening. His northern New Mexican background qualifies him to write wisely about the unique and deep spirituality in that part of the Hispanic world. Furthermore, this book incorporates the salient events of the last fifteen years and details the process by which Hispanics, soon to be the majority of Catholics in the United States, discern their mission in an increasingly multicultural church.

The first edition, published in 1990, was particularly welcome at a time when not much was available on the history of Hispanic Catholics in the United States. A group of historians and other writers had produced *Fronteras* in 1983, a first attempt to present a historical account of Hispanic Catholicism. The project of *Fronteras* originated with a team of church historians from Latin America, the Comisión de Estudios de la Historia de la Iglesia en América Latina (CEHILA), under the leadership of Dr. Enrique Dussel. Dr. Dussel convinced Fr.

Virgilio Elizondo, founding president of the Mexican American Cultural Center (MACC), to gather Hispanic writers to share papers on periods of the history of the church and Hispanics in the United States. The plan was that these papers would be published as a volume to be included in a collection of histories of the various geographical areas of the church in the Americas, including the United States.

At the MACC gathering Dr. Dussel presented the CEHILA approach to church history. It avoids any hint of triumphalism and does not simply chronicle church events. Many histories of the church are about bishops and their accomplishments. These histories are often made up of a series of chapters, each dedicated to the term of an individual bishop. CEHILA writers look at epochs according to significant political, economic, and cultural trends or movements, how these have an impact on the life of the church, and how the church responds.

CEHILA aims at writing a history from the perspective of the poor and those who have suffered oppression, different from those histories written from the vantage point of the victors and those who wield economic, military, political, or ecclesiastical power. Following the ecumenical spirit of the Second Vatican Council, CEHILA also writes from an ecumenical stance and includes the history of the Protestant church among Hispanics.

The team of Hispanic writers accepted Dr. Dussel's challenge and set out to write the chapters of the book that was given the name *Fronteras*. Thanks to Moises Sandoval, who served as editor, *Fronteras* was eventually published. It had various drawbacks, among which was a lack of consistency, often the case when several writers are involved in a common project. Also lacking, among other areas, was the story of Cuban Americans and their part in the developing story of the church in this country.

When CEHILA initiated an additional project of writing and publishing *historias mínimas* of the history of the church in the Americas by countries, Sandoval began his work on *On the Move*. His background in the field of Catholic journalism, especially his work as editor of *Maryknoll Magazine* and *Revista Maryknoll*, made him eminently qualified for the task.

This book holds the church in the United States accountable for its approaches to the Hispanic presence in many areas, particularly in the area of social concern. While the language is critical, it is not condemnatory; the author clearly writes from a knowledgeable appreciation of past events and holds church leadership accountable for its prophetic mission. This is especially true in his treatment of twentieth-century events.

Any treatment of Hispanic peoples, whether historical, political, social, or cultural, runs into the challenge presented by the wide variety within the total Hispanic spectrum. Geography is greatly responsible for this. The Spanish missions in northern New Mexico, for example, because of their location far from the mainstream and from the political centers of power of church life, necessarily developed a unique flavor and style of church spirituality. The Caribbean church maintained strong, close ties to Spain well into the twentieth century. Puerto Rican Catholics, whether in New York or on the Island, have had an experience of church quite different from that of other Hispanic Americans. The Cuban American experience also deserves special treatment, especially the events leading to and beyond the immigration experience of the 1960s.

The struggle of Hispanic Americans to maintain their cultural-religious character has gone hand in hand with the socio-economic political struggle. This book presents a saga still in the making of a people who, like other identifiable ethnic groups, has had to overcome the challenges of discrimination and racial prejudice. Unfortunately, the institutional church has not always been there to champion the causes of justice and civil rights among minorities, including those of Hispanics. Individuals in leadership positions and some religious communities in the first half of the twentieth century did take heroic stands, but it was not until the 1940s that the church, as a national and regional institution, began to recognize its role and participate in the struggle.

There are parts of this book that are not pleasant to read, but what is offered here is of vital importance if we are to avoid the pitfalls of the past. Knowing Moises Sandoval and his contributions to the life of the church over many years as a Catholic journalist, I know of his deep love and respect for the church, including its hierarchy. He writes a strong line, but out of an equally strong regard for the church's present and future, to which this generation of Catholic leadership has been responding.

This book has become the main source of the study of Hispanic church history in the United States for those preparing for ministry and others. Its small size makes it accessible, both in price and in readership, to many people. It is my prayer and hope that this book will find wide readership, and that it will continue to promote documentation, research, and writing on the topic that is as fascinating as it is challenging.

Most Rev. Ricardo Ramírez, CSB
Bishop of Las Cruces, New Mexico

Acknowledgments

I am grateful, first of all, that in 1919 my grandfather Enrique Perea built a one-room log school on his own farm in the remote foothill community of Terromote in northern New Mexico so that his children, grandchildren, and neighbors could learn to read and write and get acquainted with math, history, and geography. He opened up horizons of learning for us in other ways; he had books in his attic that we explored, and he subscribed to newspapers and periodicals that he shared with my parents and neighbors. Though my parents attended only that one-room school, they saw each day as a golden opportunity to learn something new and constantly conveyed that optimism to us, their ten children.

I am grateful as well to Father Miguel d'Escoto, my former director at Maryknoll, who first urged me to write the history of our Hispanic church, and to the Alicia Patterson Foundation, which in 1977 gave me a fellowship to spend a year researching the history of our people. Many friends and colleagues in the Commission for Historical Studies of the Church in Latin America taught me how to write history, especially noted historians Dr. Enrique Dussel of Mexico City and Father José Oscar Beozzo of Brazil.

Bishop Ricardo Ramírez of Las Cruces, a long-time friend, always encouraged me to publish my work. Father Robert Wright of Oblate School of Theology and Father Juan Romero made many helpful suggestions. Father Virgilio Elizondo provided many writing opportunities. Peggy Ellsberg and her husband, Robert, editor in chief of Orbis, helped me organize the content and smooth out the narrative of the first edition.

Finally, I could not have dedicated the evenings, weekends, and travel necessary to produce this modest work without the steadfast support of Penny, my wife, friend, and companion. In 2005 we celebrated our fiftieth wedding anniversary.

Introduction

This book is an updated and improved edition of *On the Move: A History of the Hispanic Church in the United States*, published in 1990. Reprinted four times, it met a strong need, and although it has been out of print for years, it is still being used in electronic form in university and seminary classrooms, demonstrating the continuing appeal of a compact history of the Hispanic church.

This book is divided into four parts. The first part deals with indigenous contributions of Hispanic faith; the second with conquest and evangelization by Spain; the third with the American conquest and the melting-pot church; and the fourth with the coming age of the church of the poor. I hesitated before settling on that name, for most Hispanics are not materially poor, although nearly one-third of them fall in that category, higher than for most other groups. But they are poor in the sense that, real or perceived, there is still a social distance between them and mainstream Catholics. They still lack a voice in the decision-making of the church, still lack a proportionate presence in all categories of institutional church leadership, and still have the sense they are seen as interlopers. In my parish in suburban New York, where I have been a member for thirty-five years, a man last year rather pointedly turned away rather than give me the handshake of peace during Mass. Though these snubs are much rarer than in the past, we Hispanics still remain outsiders in many ways.

Still, much has changed in the past fifteen years. During that time the Hispanic population has doubled, rising from 22 million in 1990 to 40.4 million in 2005, according to the Census

Bureau. In places like Los Angeles County, destination of heavy immigration, the Hispanic population has gone from being mostly native born to overwhelmingly foreign born. Parishes that in 1990 offered Mass in Spanish in school basements now celebrate Mass in the main parish church. In a New Jersey diocese where Puerto Ricans in the 1960s were forced to attend Mass in a chicken house, they and other Hispanics now worship in the cathedral. In other parishes, like one in Othello, Washington, the congregation for English Masses is sparse and distinctly gray haired, while that for Spanish Masses overflows to the vestibule and even outside with mothers, fathers, grandparents—and children playing in the aisles.

The prediction that Hispanics will become the majority of Catholics in the United States is about to come true, causing some unease among mainstream Catholics. But dozens of dioceses are already overwhelmingly Hispanic, with no ill effects, including the largest one, Los Angeles, where Hispanics are 65 percent of the faithful. In many places in the Southwest, the traditional region of Hispanic settlement and evangelization, the church has always been Hispanic.

I grew up in such a place in a remote rural community nestled in the foothills of the Sangre de Cristo Mountains in New Mexico. The parish was so large that the priest came to our chapel, San Isidro, to celebrate Mass only a few times a year. The parish church, Our Lady of Guadalupe, was only nine miles away, but the people had only horse-drawn wagons to take them there, and the red-clay road leading to the church was impassable after heavy rains and winter snows. Yet, my grandfather Enrique Perea felt the obligation of Sunday worship so keenly that when he could not take his family in the wagon, he went on horseback. An early rising farmer, he was already tilling his fields when the sun came up. At noon, after the main meal of the day, he would sit in his rocking chair and pray the Rosary. Today, as then, regardless of what ethnic group they claim as their own, Hispanics profess the central tenets of the faith, are conservative in its interpretation and application, and are loyal to tradition, to their church's leaders, and to its institutions.

In Terromote families knelt down each night to pray the Rosary. Lay persons, including members of the Pious Brotherhood of Our Lord Christ the Nazarene, commonly known as the Penitentes, conducted liturgies in the chapels and at funerals. They provided aid to families in need; there was no public assistance then. And when a neighbor got sick and could not tend to his crops and livestock, they and other neighbors came to his aid. Tuberculosis was a great scourge, leaving many orphans, but relatives always took them in. Their community spirit would be the envy of the best-served urban parish today.

Thanks to the research stimulated by the 1992 Fifth Centenary observance, we now have a clearer picture of the indigenous roots of Hispanic Catholicism in the New World. Pope John Paul II took a historic step in 2002 when, in a ceremony at the basilica of Our Lady of Guadalupe in Mexico City, he canonized Juan Diego, the Náhuatl Indian peasant to whom the Blessed Virgin, according to tradition, appeared in 1531. It was the beginning of recognition five hundred years overdue: that indigenous people have contributed in many ways to the spirit and belief of Catholicism in the New World and that this enriches rather than contaminates their faith. Historically, the church had seen nothing of value in indigenous religion, condemning it as worship of demons, or worse, of the devil.

However, theologians now see the parallels in the quest for God of indigenous cultures and that of cultures in the Middle East and Europe. Indigenous cultures in the Americas were traveling paths followed earlier by their conquerors. As a Dominican priest concluded, Indians already believed in God when Europeans arrived; the only new elements Europeans brought were those of Christ and the gospel. Therefore, while as recently as forty years ago the fusion of Indian and Christian belief was seen as proof of inadequate evangelization, the church has begun to see it as enriching. Though not considered in depth in this volume, the same can be said of the mixture of

Christianity and African belief found in Caribbean Hispanic people. Hispanics bring more than the traditional Catholicism from Europe. The faith of Hispanics in the United States, wrote Mexican novelist Carlos Fuentes, contains the idea that the world is holy, which he called one of the oldest and deepest truths in the Amerindian world.

Since the first edition of *On The Move* was published, Hispanic theologians representing Mexicans, Cubans, Puerto Ricans, Dominicans, Central Americans, and South Americans, Catholics as well as Protestants, have produced a rich harvest of writing on culture and pluralism, feminist liberation, tradition and symbol, popular religion, *mestizaje*, prayer, worship, and liturgy. While twenty years ago San Antonio diocesan priest Virgil Elizondo was the sole highly visible Hispanic theologian, now there are scores, many of them women, producing many theological works grounded in the historical experience of their people, formerly marginalized and voiceless.

New histories, regional as well as national, have appeared. While historians were few when we first began in 1975 under the auspices of the Commission for Historical Studies of the Church in Latin America (CEHILA), now there are many. In the past fifteen years they have published a three-volume *Notre Dame History of Hispanic Catholics*; *¡Presente! U.S. Latino Catholics from Colonial Times to the Present*; *Oxcart Catholicism on Fifth Avenue: The Impact of the Puerto Rican Migration upon the Archdiocese of New York*; and many other works.

Liturgists wrote and published many new hymns and recovered many traditional ones shunned when the mainstream church was trying to ladle Hispanics into the melting pot. Centers for Hispanic ministry endured and prospered, and new institutes and organizations appeared, like the National Catholic Council for Hispanic ministry (NCCHM), established in the 1990s. Hispanic ministers began to look beyond serving their own people to serving the mainstream church as well. Although Hispanic leadership in the institutional church remained static, with no significant increase in bishops, clergy, religious women, and lay ministers, Hispanic leaders ministered, as in the past, not so much individually but through the witness of families, groups, and communities as a whole: the Penitentes of New Mexico, the martyrs of Central America during the violent decades of the 1970s and 1980s, the sacrifices made by Cesar Chavez, the unshakable faith of countless families that God will provide.

A Hispanic church is clearly taking form, with brown faces in the pews, fresh hymns coming from the choir, organizations and institutions teaching an evangelizing mission, and a new theology guiding its journey. At the same time, the mainstream is redirecting energy and resources to its burgeoning Hispanic membership and learning Spanish; that is where the church's future is. Demographers say the growth of the Catholic population in the United States in the next fifty years will come only from Hispanics, native born and foreign born, and other immigrants. The fertility of the mainstream population has declined to replacement level, part of a trend demographers also see in Europe. It seems the time of *la raza* is finally arriving!

Part I

Contributions
of Pre-Columbian Religion

Chapter 1

The Indigenous Heritage

In 2002 at the Basilica of Our Lady of Guadalupe in Mexico City Pope John Paul II canonized Juan Diego a saint—recognition almost five hundred years overdue. But the legacy of Guadalupe and hence the debt was due not just to the simple Indian peasant to whom, according to tradition, the Blessed Virgin Mary appeared in 1531. It was due to the many generations of Náhuatl Indians who nourished the tradition of Guadalupe before the Spaniards began to document it more than a century after the apparitions. The story of Guadalupe was told, danced, transmitted from mouth to mouth and from people to people before it was written and accepted by the church.[1] The original account of Guadalupe, a collective work of Indian theologians, was penned in the Náhuatl language by an Indian who had studied and taught at the Colegio de La Santa Cruz de Tlatelolco, then directed by Indians. The belated canonization of Juan Diego only begins to acknowledge the history, presence, role, and value of Indian religion in the Catholicism the Spaniards planted in the Americas.

Indian religion permeates the faith of Hispanic Catholics in the Americas, and its paradigm is Guadalupe. Guadalupe, however, is just one of many Indian gifts to the American church. The Cuban devotion to Our Lady of Charity began when two Taino Indians, Juan and Rodrigo de Hoyos, and a black slave boy, Juan Moreno, found a miraculous statue of the Virgin floating in Nipe Bay near the northwestern tip of Cuba in 1610. The Santuario of Chimayo, the most popular pilgrimage destination in New Mexico, links a sacred Indian site with a Christian tradition. The Santuario, visited annually by pilgrims from throughout the Southwest, was built over a spring sacred to the Indians for its healing properties. Research on other devotions and pilgrimage sites would doubtless reveal similar links with indigenous religion.

Religion for Hispanics in the United States, wrote Mexican novelist Carlos Fuentes,[2] includes not only Catholicism but also the idea that the world is holy, which he called one of the oldest truths in the Amerindian world. In Hispanic popular religion, defined as the religion of the people, the natural and supernatural realms become closely intertwined. Father Daniel Groody, CSC, a theologian who studied the religious practices and spirituality of Mexican farm workers in California, concluded that pre-Columbian religion, especially the ability to contemplate, flows in their veins: "They know they are in the presence of the holy."[3] The popular devotions of Hispanics, according to theologian Juan Schobinger, are based "more on indigenous cultural elements than on official Roman Catholic worship patterns." Moreover, the cosmovision of Hispanic Catholics, like that of indigenous peoples, "is intuitive rather than rational, open to nature instead of blinded by ego, communitarian rather than individualistic, in which all that is visible symbolized a greater reality on whom everyone depends."[4]

The religious history of the Hispanic people of the United States begins with the faith journey of people who crossed the Bering Strait to Alaska twelve thousand years ago. Over several thousand years, as they migrated to the tip of South America, indigenous people heard God speaking to them, as God speaks to every culture. They responded in faith and practice according to their understanding of that message, parts of which are alive in Hispanic faith today. These Indian beliefs were incorporated into Iberian Catholicism, already different from that in the rest of Europe, blending elements of Christian, Jewish, and

Arab religions and cultures. To that already multiracial and multicultural religion, the millions of slaves brought to the Americas beginning in the fifteenth century added their contribution, especially in the Caribbean. Their devotional and spiritual practices incorporate African beliefs and devotions, one of them Santeria.

There is no written history of the evolution of religion in the Americas; only a small elite in Mesoamerica possessed the art of writing. Archeology nevertheless yields substantial evidence. Drawings, etchings, symbols, sculptures, ceramics, pyramids, and prayer platforms reveal the search for God, the rise of religious leaders, and the development of ritual and cult. Shamanism, which arose among the Ural-Altaic peoples of northern Europe and Asia, also appeared in the Americas, seeking to explain an unseen world of gods, demons, and ancestral spirits. Suggesting the same origins, stone and ceramic drawings and etchings in the Americas resemble those found in caves in France and Spain going back to Paleolithic times.

Like other peoples across the globe, the first inhabitants of the Americas perceived the need to serve God, do penance and offer sacrifice, choose good and reject evil, see the hand of God in all creation and live a moral life in harmony with their family and community. The mountaintop, a sacred place going back in ancient Palestine at least to the time of Abraham, was also holy for indigenous peoples, who built their prayer platforms on hilltops and mountaintops. The pyramids built by the Mayas were a symbolic outreach to the cosmos. Their interest in the stars enabled the Mayas to develop mathematical concepts more advanced than those of the Greeks and to craft the most accurate calendar in the world during that era. To this day four sacred peaks anchor Navajo religion in the US southwest.

Similarly, Christians and indigenous people envisioned heaven, or at least the abode of God, as being in the sky and the abode of the devil, or of evil, as being underground. In the cosmovision of Mesoamerica, the universe had thirteen heavens superimposed on one another, each with its own god.

There were nine subterranean worlds, the deepest one belonging to the god of death. Some gods were good, such as those of rain and fertility; others were bad, such as those of drought, tempest, and war. For Andean people, the earth itself was God, the mother who brought forth and sustained life. They prayed to her for fertility of the land, safety for travelers, a good birth for mothers, and happiness in all enterprises. A similar idea of God existed at one time in Eurasia.

The Pueblo Indians of what is now the southwestern United States worshiped some spirits and feared others. Their ceremonial life had frequent rituals. They believed supernatural forces controlled their lives and had to be propitiated to ensure success in hunting and farming and to ward off illness or enemies. The *kachina* cult represented supernatural beings that may have been ancestral spirits. The people worshiped a supreme being, the sun god of the nomads but equally the mother earth of the planters. The jaguar, god of the hunters, had a special place in their pantheon.

Nevertheless, some groups had arrived at the realization that there is only one god. The Taino peoples of the Caribbean had a supreme being "who is in heaven and whom nobody can see and who has a mother, but no beginning."[5] They named their god Yocohu Baque Moorócoti, and his mother, Atabey. With the hindsight of five hundred years, a Dominican priest, a modern-day spiritual descendant of one of the first missionary orders in the Americas, wrote: "The Taino Indians believed in God; the only new element the Spaniards added was that of Christ and the Gospel."[6]

For the Mayas of Mexico and Central America, Hunab was the creator of the world and his son Itzmna was the lord of the skies, of night and day, and the hero of civilization because he gave the Mayas the art of writing and the calendar. Other cultures—there were thousands of them—had many gods.

There were hundreds of tribes on lands now in the United States, hunter-gatherers on the Pacific Coast, planters in the Southwest and Southeast. The political organization of a particular tribe was simple; it had one or more chiefs. There were associations of various kinds of warriors, the leaders of religious rituals and ceremonies, the medicine men, the heads of various totemic cults, animal or mineral. The style of life was communal. In most tribes the basic unit of society was a monogamous family, though there were a few tribes that practiced polygamy. For the most part, their broad sense of social morality—on such questions as murder or adultery or slavery, for example—was similar to that of their conquerors. Their world view consisted of a cosmic dualism. Spring struggled against winter, the sun against the moon. There were spirits and demons, and numerous mythologies.

Prairie Indians, who lived west of the Mississippi, divided their camps and villages into two parts, representing earth and sky. The sky was the masculine principle, the earth the feminine. There was a supreme being, the organizer of the land. For some, the earth, as in Andean cultures, was the supreme being.

The pueblos had guilds or associations for healers, hunters, warriors, and religious and social leaders. The religious associations carried out the ceremonial life, usually in *kivas*—large worship chambers for unmarried males. They believed life after death would be similar to life on earth. They could not accept that as a consequence of how they lived on earth, they could be tortured in hell for all eternity.

As in other parts of the world, priests led ritual, cult, and ceremony; interpreted cosmic and religious phenomena; and served as arbiters of personal and social morality. Some cultures had a variety of ministers, from shamans to warrior priests to sacrificers, cult leaders, and medicine men. In some groups the priesthood was a powerful class able to mobilize the resources, skills, and labor to build elaborate temples, pyramids, and at times, entire complexes of buildings, plazas, monoliths, and sculptures. At Teotihuacan, thirty miles northeast of present-day Mexico City, the Olmecs could not have built the massive pyramids to the sun and to the moon and their surrounding structures without the support of political and economic leaders.

In such advanced cultures priests were among the powerful elite who could read and write and who possessed other skills. As in Europe, such power came in exchange for identifying with the goals of political and military leaders.

Had they come with an open mind, the European newcomers could have found many coincidences and convergences between their faith and that of the indigenous inhabitants. Harmony and a common spirit animated both traditions. Pablo Richard, a theologian from Costa Rica, sees in indigenous religions the structure of the history of salvation found in the Bible. The Bible and indigenous religious tradition converge on the recognition of Yahweh as God, the Exodus, the continual remembrance of the stories of ancestors, the fundamental myths to reinforce identity and historical conscience to confront oppression, the struggle for land, and the historical and narrative character of theology.[7]

Traditions similar to that of Jesus, prophet and teacher, exist among all indigenous peoples. In Mesoamerica that figure is Quetzalcoatl, peaceful and long-suffering; among the Kuna of Panama, it is Ibeorgun. The Christian belief that God sent his only son to take human form and be crucified for the redemption of humanity has its parallel in Olmec culture. These people believed that at Teotihuacan (meaning "city of the gods"), the god Nanahuatzin threw himself in the fire and thereby created the sun. In that way the gods created the present world and the human race. The people therefore made offerings, at times human sacrifices, to atone in some way for the sun's original sacrifice. In the duality of life and death in indigenous religions, which historian Osvaldo Silva describes as the "union of contraries,"[8] death is seen as transformation and the seed of new life. Similarly, by his death and resurrection Christ brought new life to humanity.

Human sacrifices by the Aztecs, abhorred by the conquistadors, had also occurred in their tradition. In ancient Palestine, Abraham attempted to sacrifice his only son, Isaac, and though

God held back his hand, the practice did not end, though sacrifices of animals and the fruits of the harvest were more common. In pagan times during a time of famine in Sweden the chieftains first sacrificed oxen, then, when the crops did not improve, human beings, and finally, King Domald.[9] The Mass, which the Europeans brought to the Americas, commemorates the sacrifice of God's own son on the cross.

Notwithstanding the many convergences, Europeans failed to see that many indigenous beliefs and practices were connected in some way to the origins of their own religious outlook. No doubt the early Christians would have been more receptive, when religion was communal and open to all. But five hundred years ago, in an age of religious warfare, all peoples were either believers or infidels. Europeans saw all indigenous religion as idolatry or, worse, as worship of the devil. Attempting to crush it, they defaced and destroyed temples and other places of worship and punished severely, even executing, those who refused to give up their beliefs. Europeans believed they were the sole custodians of the word of God. To this day a religiosity with elements from other traditions is considered defective, less than authentic.

Yet, the times are changing. Because modern humanity has polluted the earth's air and waters, built enough nuclear weapons to destroy the planet many times over, despoiled its most precious resources, and even tampered with its genetic codes, the Indian idea that the world is holy appeals to religious leaders as the foundation for a new theology of the environment. The ability of indigenous peoples to experience joy even in the face of appalling living conditions and the strength to be able to survive burdens that would crush other cultures have similar appeal.

In time, the syncretic nature of Hispanic religion will be seen as its strength.

Part II

Conquest and Evangelization
by the Spaniards

Chapter 2

Conquest, Settlement, and Evangelization

A rrival of Europeans in the New World led to a conquest not seen before or since. Of its three parts, biological, military, and religious, the first was the worst. In one century the Indian population declined from 54 million to 10 million, a catastrophe from which indigenous people never recovered. The population has grown so slowly in the last four hundred years that in 1992 there were only 63 million indigenous people in the Americas. During that time the descendants of the 15 million black slaves brought to the New World beginning in the sixteenth century multiplied almost ten times, to 140 million. Clearly, after five hundred years, life remains precarious for the original inhabitants of the Americas, suggesting that the conquest begun five hundred years ago has yet to end.

The Indians were decimated by what in today's parlance might be called the mother of all biological wars. Though not intentional, it was no less deadly. In their bodies Europeans brought the germs of the major killer diseases of humans: smallpox, flu, tuberculosis, typhus, malaria, plague, measles, and cholera. Having no immunity, the Indians became ill and began to die from the first encounters with the invaders. Smallpox killed nearly half of the Aztecs, including Emperor Cuitláhuac, after the first Spanish attack in 1520. By the time

Francisco Pizarro and the Incas faced each other in the field of battle, smallpox had already killed the emperor and most of his court. The indigenous people had no comparable diseases to decimate the Europeans.

When Fernando de Soto explored the Carolinas, Georgia, Alabama, and Louisiana in 1538 he found town sites abandoned when the inhabitants died two years earlier in epidemics of diseases brought by Spaniards who had visited the coast. More than a century later, when European (French) settlers next came to the area, almost all of the big Indian towns had disappeared.[1] Diseases there and in many other areas of the Americas killed up to 95 percent of the native population. The Indian population of Hispaniola declined from about eight million in 1492 to zero[2] in 1535, that of Cuba from 100,000 in 1492 to 14,000 in 1532. What's more, there and elsewhere, the decline continued for several centuries. In New Mexico there were about forty thousand natives when Juan de Oñate and his colonists arrived in 1598, but only sixteen thousand remained in 1680 when the Indians revolted. In California, there were seventy-two thousand Indians when Fray Junipero Serra began the first missions in 1769; only fifteen thousand remained in 1836.

Military Conquest

Unequal military warfare also decimated the natives. The invaders had swords, lances, and daggers made of steel, as well as small firearms and artillery; the natives had only bows and arrows and clubs and axes made of stone. The conquistadors had steel helmets and body armor of steel or chain mail; the Indians wore only quilted garments. The Spaniards had horses, a major weapon of warfare for six thousand years. The natives had no horses or other animals they could use in combat; they had to fight on foot.

The Indians had no large animals that could have been domesticated to pull plows, transport goods, or provide animal protein; such animals had become extinct in the Americas during an ice age of the Late Pleistocene period. They domesticated only the llama, an animal of limited utility found only in the Andes. Unlike the horse, it could not be used as a vehicle for warfare or to pull a plow. Eurasia, however, had been able to domesticate thirteen species of animals to provide meat, milk, wool, and hides; transport goods and serve as vehicles of war; pull plows or turn grinding wheels; and provide manure to fertilize crops. The germs that decimated the peoples of the New World had evolved from the diseases of these animals.

Eurasia also had most of the world's large-grained, protein-rich wild cereals and had domesticated them thousands of years before the people of the Americas were able to domesticate their smaller-grained cereals and corn, which is not rich in protein. Food production enabled the peoples of Eurasia to evolve from hunter-gatherers to establish villages, then cities, and finally, nation states. With abundant food production, part of the labor force could develop new technologies, crafts, skills, and enterprises. Among them, Eurasians found practical uses for the wheel: wheelbarrows, carts, windmills, and grinding wheels. In the New World wheels were found only on Mexican ceramic toys.

By the Middle Ages most of Eurasia had organized into nation states; in the Americas only two, the Aztecs and the Incas, could mobilize resources on the same scale in 1492. European leaders and in some states part of the general population could read and write. In the Americas only a small elite in Mesoamerica was literate. The powerful Incas had only an accounting system, a mnemonic device based on knots.[3] The invaders therefore had the advantage of thousands of years of written history, including the history of warfare.

The huge disparities led to the belief, still held by many today, that Eurasian cultures were innately superior to those of the Americas. But, in fact, the inhabitants of Eurasia were more fortunate. Since Europe and Asia are in the same climate zone, plants and fruits domesticated in the Fertile Crescent could also be cultivated in Europe and China. Communication, transportation, and commerce were much easier in Eurasia, while the north-south axis of the Americas had many climatic, ecological, and geographical barriers. Moreover, humans had inhabited Eurasia for one million years as compared to only twelve thousand years in the Americas.

Since the first goal of the conquest was to acquire riches, the prime targets were the two advanced societies, the Aztecs and the Incas. They possessed gold, silver, and precious stones, and they had skills the invaders could utilize: expertise in architecture, construction, hydraulics, agriculture, and working with stone, ceramics, and copper. They also had buildings and other properties useful to the Europeans. Moreover, by defeating their rulers, the Spaniards gained control over vast territories.

Elsewhere the military conquest was not as permanent or as complete as the biological conquest. For the Indians who lived beyond Aztec influence in the rest of North America, poverty provided a reprieve for at least a century. Soon after conquering the Aztecs and the Incas, the conquistadors came to lands now in the United States looking for rich kingdoms; finding none, they lost interest in settlement and conquest for half a century.

Since the estimated twenty million natives in North America were divided into hundreds of tribes with many language groups, conquest was difficult. There were six major cultural groups, excluding the Inuit, located in the Northwest, the plains, the plateaus, the Eastern Woodlands, the northern area, and the Southwest. The main language groups were the Aztec-Tanoan, Algonquian-Wakashan, and the Hokan-Siouan, but with many variations. East of the Mississippi the Spaniards met the Caddos, Muscogi, and Timicua; in the high plains, the Wichitas and the Comanches; in the Southwest, pueblo tribes like the Zuni and the Tewa, the Apache and the Papago.

In the Southwest the Cochise (c. 8000 BCE), the earliest known inhabitants, gave way to the Mogollon. Between 5000 and 1000 BCE, manioc, maize, beans, and squash were domesticated in both North and South America. The Pueblos, who reached their zenith between 1300 and 900 BCE, were prosperous and well organized, the men and women modestly dressed. They were skilled weavers and potters, makers of turquoise and coral jewelry. One of their ethnic branches built the fabled seven cities of Cibola, of which only Acoma remains. Life for all the Indians living in territories now part of the United States was elemental—a struggle for land, food and security. Warfare with other tribes was constant.

Because they were the most settled and not as warlike as other groups, the Pueblos were the most vulnerable. The Spaniards put them to work growing crops and raising livestock or fighting hostile tribes. In New Mexico many Pueblo Indians fought for the Spaniards. Eventually, though, as had happened in Puerto Rico, Cuba, and Georgia, the weight of the conquest became too heavy and the Pueblo Indians revolted. In 1680 they killed 380 settlers and 21 missionaries and forced the survivors to retreat south to El Paso. The Spaniards returned in force a dozen years later and conquered the territory again, hanging scores of the Indian leaders.

Even with Indian help, the conquistadors subjugated few of the indigenous peoples. After two hundred years, they still controlled only pockets of territory, even in the Southwest. The area was too vast, the tribes too numerous, the terrain too inhospitable or remote, and the conquerors were too few. Peace, when it existed with any group, was always tenuous. Missions might operate for a time, only to be overrun by a new uprising. This was true everywhere, but particularly in Texas and Arizona. Time did not improve the chances of conquest. As horses became available to the Indians, they were able to fight on more even terms. More important, some tribes previously sedentary reverted to a nomadic life, following the buffalo herds. Putting the Indians to work for Europeans became more difficult.

Nevertheless, wherever Indians were under the control of the Spaniards, they suffered under the *encomienda* system, legalized in 1503 and utilized first in the Caribbean. Indians were given to Spanish military officers, political leaders, and missionaries, a practice that later became hereditary, thereby becoming virtual slavery. Indians were forced to work cultivating crops, raising livestock, building the missions and churches, and working as servants in households.

Exploration

Spaniards came to lands now in the United States in search of gold even before the Aztecs and Incas were conquered. When Juan Ponce de Leon, conqueror of Puerto Rico, landed in Florida near the present site of St. Augustine on April 2, 1513, he had already enriched himself from the gold discovered on the Island. Though legend has it that he was looking for the fountain of youth on the island of Bimeni, more likely he was in quest of more gold. Because it was the Easter season, he named the new land La Gran Pascua Florida, the Spanish name for the feast of Easter.

Finding the Indians hostile, the Spaniards reboarded their ships and sailed south along the coast of Florida—which they took to be an island—and then sailed north on the western coast, where they also landed briefly. Returning to Puerto Rico, Ponce de Leon soon afterward sailed for Spain, where he received a patent to colonize Florida. His commission directed him to submit the Indians to the Catholic faith and to the authority of the Spanish crown. When he returned to Puerto Rico, Indian conflicts delayed him, and he did not set out on a second expedition until 1521. With two hundred men and fifty horses he landed on the west coast of Florida, probably near present-day Tampa. But Indians immediately attacked, and an arrow wounded Ponce de Leon. Abandoning the project, the expedition went to Cuba, where Ponce de Leon died.

In 1527 Pánfilo de Narvaez landed on the gulf coast of Florida with six hundred colonists and several Franciscan missioners looking for a rich kingdom. One half of his men marched inland under his command while the other half continued by ship. Returning to the coast empty-handed, Narvaez and his men could not find the ships. They therefore constructed makeshift boats to return home. But they were driven off course and shipwrecked on Galveston Island, off the Texas coast, where the Indians enslaved the survivors.

Ten years later, in 1538, visions of gold also led Hernando de Soto to Tampa Bay. He explored what is now the southeastern United States. Wounded in a battle with the Indians, he died on May 21, 1542, as the expedition reached the Mississippi River. He was buried on its banks, but his men went on to visit lands now known as Arkansas, Texas, and Oklahoma.

Meanwhile, after being enslaved by Indians for seven years on Galveston Island, four survivors of the Narvaez expedition escaped to the mainland. Alvar Núñez Cabeza de Vaca, Alonso del Castillo Maldonado, Andrés Dorantes, and an Arab or black identified only as Estevánico walked across Texas, New Mexico, Arizona, and northern Mexico. When they arrived in Culiacan in 1536, they reported the Indians had told them of a kingdom called Cibola with seven cities possessing great riches. In 1539 Fray Marcos de Niza, accompanied by Estevánico, returned from a visit to New Mexico with the news that they had actually seen one of the fabled seven cities of Cibola.

Once again dreaming of gold the Spaniards, led by Francisco Vasquez de Coronado, assembled an expedition of three hundred Spaniards and eight hundred Indian allies. In 1540 they marched north in search of Cibola. For two years they explored lands now known as Arizona, New Mexico, Oklahoma, and Kansas, but they found only poor Indian villages and not the rich kingdom envisioned with such anticipation as a "new Mexico." That ended the quest for gold on lands now in the United States. For half a century afterward the Spaniards showed no further interest in New Mexico.

In September 1542, as Coronado returned to Mexico from the plains empty-handed, Juan Rodríguez de Cabrillo discovered the Bay of San Diego, and in 1602 Sebastian Vizcaino discovered the Bay of Monterey, both in California. Settlement, however, would have to wait more than two hundred years. These explorers had no inkling of the gold that would one day be discovered in California.

Colonization

Although missionaries always came along, most Spanish colonies north of Mexico were founded primarily for political reasons. In 1565, when Pedro Menéndez de Aviles established St. Augustine at the mouth of the St. John River on the east coast of Florida, the Spaniards' first permanent colony on lands now in the United States, Spain was trying to keep France out of the peninsula, having destroyed a French fort there the previous year. Their interests secured, the Spaniards did not start their second settlement, this one in Pensacola, until 1696. They eventually founded about a dozen settlements in Florida.

Earlier, six hundred colonists headed by Captain Lucas Vasquez de Ayllon had in 1526 attempted to establish a colony alongside Chesapeake Bay, but a pestilential fever and a revolt by Indian and black slaves killed many of the colonists, including Ayllon. The 150 who survived returned to Hispaniola in 1527.

French incursions in the region now called East Texas led Spaniards to order Alonso de Leon and Fray Damian Massanet to build the mission of San Francisco de Los Tejas on May 25, 1690, and a second mission a year later. Similarly, Russians pushing down from Alaska spurred the Spaniards to build the twenty-one California missions and other settlements beginning in 1769.

Similar concerns planted the flag and cross on lands now in the state of Washington. In 1774, a ship sailed through the Strait of Juan de Fuca and into Puget Sound, where Fray Tomas de La Peña and Fray Juan Crespi celebrated Mass for the first time in that region. In July 1775 the Spaniards built a small colony on the Olympic Peninsula.[4] Though it apparently no longer existed in 1800, Spain claimed that territory until 1819 when it became part of the United States through the Adams-Onis Treaty.

Only the colonization of New Mexico was free of external pressures. In 1598 Juan de Oñate led 400 settlers to New Mexico, including 138 women and children, 8 Franciscans, and 3 Mexican Indians who had not taken their final vows. It was the first expedition that included women and children. On the feast of the Ascension, near present-day El Paso, he took possession of the area for God and King Philip of Spain. It would become the most populous, and the most enduring, Spanish colony in the United States.

Evangelization

Evangelization by Spain, historian Enrique Dussel writes, was not simply an expansion of religion but a complete change of system, political, economic, and cultural. An inglorious and ambiguous process, it justified violent conquest, continuing a long history of religious warfare going back to the year 718, when Spain began its eight-century struggle to expel the Moors. When they finally succeeded, in 1492, war against the "infidels" transformed itself into war against the indigenous peoples of the Americas.[5] Spaniards saw religion as an interminable conflict between the kingdom of God and the dominion of the devil. As leaders of the Inquisition and the Counter-Reformation, Spaniards felt called to evangelize and had no compunction about using force to do so.

Indians with gold were considered fortunate because they would hear the word of God (after being conquered and deprived of their gold and other riches) and thus be saved from eternal damnation. In the famous document *El Parecer de Yucay*, Fray García de Toledo argued: "If there is no gold, there is no

God in the Indies." Five hundred years later Peruvian theologian Gustavo Gutiérrez marveled at that reverse Christology; Christ, after all, came to preach the gospel to the poor.[6] Nevertheless, by the time the indigenous survivors heard the gospel, they were not only poor but virtual slaves. To this day the richest parishes, communities, and families get the best evangelization. For example, excepting the few students on special scholarships, an education at the best Catholic universities requires wealth (that is, gold).

The dreams of gold in Florida had died, however, when in 1549 Dominican Friar Luis Cancer de Barbastro launched an expedition seeking the spiritual conquest of Florida. With typical bravery—or foolhardiness—Father Diego Tolsa landed without armed escort. When a companion brought word that he had been killed, Cancer jumped into the water and swam ashore. On a small rise, in full view of the crew of the ship, the Indians surrounded Cancer and killed him with knives and tomahawks as he knelt in prayer. The Dominicans made another attempt in 1555, but a hurricane sank half the ships as they headed for Pensacola.

In Texas, Indian attacks forced the Spaniards to abandon East Texas just three years after de Leon and Massanet had established San Francisco de Los Tejas and another mission in 1690. Two decades later they started six other missions in the province, not counting El Paso, Ysleta, and Socorro. In all, about twenty missions were eventually built at a cost of millions of pesos, but only those in present-day San Antonio and La Bahia endured until the nineteenth century.

Evangelization in New Mexico began in 1542 when three priests and a religious brother accompanying Coronado on his fruitless search for gold stayed behind to evangelize the Indians. All were killed except the brother, who returned to Mexico with the news of their deaths. Four decades later, in the 1580s, small groups began to venture north again. In 1581 Franciscan brother Agustín Rodríguez and fathers Francisco López and Juan de Santa María, accompanied by nine soldiers, went up the

Rio Grande looking for "a great harvest of souls." For a year they visited as far north as Taos, east to Pecos, and west to Acoma and Zuni. Returning home alone with the news of their discoveries, Santa María was killed by the Indians. In 1582 Antonio de Espejo led a small expedition to find out what had happened to the other missioners. Effective evangelization would have to wait until Oñate started a permanent colony. With an eye for wealth, Espejo reported there were good mining sites in New Mexico.

Like Coronado before him, who had executed hundreds of Indians for refusing to provide food for his expedition, Espejo did not understand that, farming by hand, the Indians had little food to spare. He executed sixteen Indians and burned others at the stake for refusing to contribute food.[7] Violence continued with Oñate, who burned Acoma pueblo in retaliation for the killing of thirteen Spaniards. Alonso de Benavides, custodian of the New Mexico missions, wrote in 1634: "So great is the fear which God has instilled in them of these few Spaniards that they do not come near where they are."[8] In various expeditions after the Pueblo revolt in 1680 expelled the Spaniards for twelve years, Diego de Vargas set fire to several Indian villages. After the reoccupation of Santa Fe in 1693, he executed seventy of the Indian leaders.

Evangelization in what is now Arizona began in 1687, led by Jesuit missionary Eusebio Kino. Working among the Pima, Papago, Yuma, and other Indians until his death in 1711, he established twenty-nine missions. Like the missions of Texas, however, they were under constant threat. In 1751 a general uprising by the Pima and Papago Indians ended many of them. Of the remaining ones, most failed when King Charles III expelled all the Jesuits from the Spanish Empire in 1767. The Franciscans took over from the Jesuits and then maintained a tenuous foothold until Arizona became part of the United States.

On July 1, 1769, Franciscans led by Junipero Serra founded Mission San Diego, the first of twenty-one missions in California, and, less than a year later, established the presidio and mission at Monterey. San Gabriel, San Luis Obispo, San Antonio, and San Carlos followed within four years. Juan Bautista de Anza marched from Tubac mission in Arizona across the California desert to San Gabriel in 1775. He explored San Francisco Bay and searched for a site for the presidio. By 1776 the San Francisco mission was going up. In economic terms the missions were a remarkable success; in 1834 they were valued at $78 million. But they generally failed to evangelize the Indians.

The basic mission structure was the *reduction*, usually encompassing villages and surrounding cultivated areas where the Indians were obliged to live and work. Reductions were common in Florida, California, Arizona, and Texas. In New Mexico, where the missionaries dealt with sedentary peoples, they usually placed the mission compound within or just outside the pueblos. Within the reductions were *repartimientos*—mines, farms, or shops—and *encomiendas*—land grants, usually given to soldiers in lieu of pay, which included the Indians to work them. Indians had to toil nine months of each year for their masters and only three for themselves.

In New Mexico during the seventeenth century the Indians were caught in a struggle for power between the missioners and the royal governors. The latter established workshops where Indian slaves captured in raids produced textiles and other goods that were then sold to enrich their masters. One governor by the name of Mendizabal (1659–69) was convicted of using slave labor to enrich himself. But many others went unpunished. The ill treatment extended to the lower castes of mixed race: the mestizos (white and Indian), the zambos (black and Indian), and the mulattoes (black and white). The missions similarly forced the Indians to work in their workshops or fields. But the oppression went beyond economic exploitation.

Evangelization attacked Indian religious belief. Instruments of worship such as masks, prayer sticks, and prayer feathers were confiscated. Indian places of worship, such as the *kivas* of the Pueblos, were destroyed or closed. The civil authorities and the army made sure the Indians obeyed the missionaries. They administered corporal punishment such as flogging and prolonged kneeling. Native religious leaders who persisted in following their beliefs were whipped or executed. That was why San Juan Tewa leader Popé and forty-six other Indian leaders were publicly whipped in Santa Fe in 1675. Five years later Popé led the Pueblo Indian revolt.

At the same time that the missionaries gave instruction in Catholic dogma, they taught Spanish and demanded respect for Spanish law and authority. To nomadic people they preached the values of sedentary life. They also demanded that the Indians accept the Spanish political system, social customs, and dress codes, and avoid drinking alcohol and using body paint. Indian women had to convert to Catholicism to have a legitimate marriage with a Spaniard. Taken all together, the program of the missionaries sought to persuade the Indians to abandon not only their religion but their culture as well.

By the Spaniards' own accounts many of the missions were a great success. In 1606 Bishop Juan Cabezas Altamirano, the first Catholic prelate to set foot on territories now in the United States, visited missions in Florida. He was apparently impressed, because the missions were elevated to a custodia in 1609 and to a province of the Diocese of Cuba in 1612. By 1634 thirty-four Franciscans worked in Florida, ministering, according to the Spaniards, to forty thousand Indians. In 1655 seventy friars worked in thirty-eight missions from St. Augustine to Georgia and west to present-day Tallahassee. Nearly two decades later, in 1674, Bishop Gabriel de Calderon spent eight months visiting the missions. He conferred minor orders on seven young men and confirmed 13,152 persons.

The reports from New Mexico were even more impressive. By 1604 the missions there had been declared a commissary, the basic organizational unit. By 1616 they had been elevated to custodia. In 1625 fourteen missionaries worked in the territory; that year the new custodian of the missions, Alonso de Benavides, brought twelve more. The colony was divided into seven missionary districts. Churches and chapels were built in the pueblos. In the larger ones there was a mission compound with workshops where the Indians were taught weaving, leatherworking, blacksmithing, and other skills. In 1630 Benavides wrote that sixty thousand Pueblo Indians in ninety villages had accepted the Catholic faith.

"All the Indians are now converted, baptized and well ministered to, with 33 convents and churches in the principal pueblos and more than 150 churches throughout the other pueblos," he reported. "Here where scarcely 30 years earlier all was idolatry and worship of the devil, without any vestige of civilization, today they worship our true God and Lord. The whole land is dotted with churches and convents and crosses along the road."[9] In California, too, the Franciscans claimed to have converted fifty-four thousand Indians during the sixty-five years those missions were in operation.

As time went on it became clear that early claims about the success of the missions had been vastly exaggerated. The Indians rebelled not only in New Mexico but also in other areas. After enduring half a century of coercive missionary work and forced labor, the Hopi and Zuni tribes killed their missionaries and returned to their ancient religious practices. The Hopi never again accepted the missionaries. In Georgia, the Guale took up arms because the missionaries forbade them to practice polygamy. When these rebellions were crushed, passive resistance continued. Some practices were accepted out of love of ritual or ceremony, but few converts abandoned their old beliefs. During the eighteenth century the Pueblo religious leaders returned to their *kivas* to worship in the old ways. After two hundred years the Pueblo Indians, those most susceptible to evangelization because of their sedentary ways, conformed to Christianity only superficially.[10]

There were, however, some success stories. The Papagos retained their Christianity even though they had no priests. The faith also took root among the Tewa Indians, who fled New Mexico with the retreating survivors of the Pueblo Revolt in 1680 and settled in El Paso. Assimilated Indians in San Antonio and other places also embraced Catholicism. But for most of the Indians, death came before conversion.

As in the rest of the New World, European diseases killed most of the Indians. Some historians consider the initial and surviving population in California and New Mexico as serious underestimates, but there is no argument about the steep decline in the number of Indian inhabitants. In Florida only a remnant of the Timucua and other tribes remained. They merged with the Seminole Indians, who moved down from Alabama and western Georgia. The decimation continued under American rule. In the second Seminole War (1835–52) the majority were killed or forcibly removed to reservations in the West. Only fifteen hundred Seminoles lived in Florida in the late twentieth century.[11]

Conflicts among Spain, France, England, and the United States made the missions prime targets. Florida was a battleground even before the Spaniards established themselves in St. Augustine in 1565. In 1702 and 1704 the British and their Indian allies destroyed the Florida missions. By 1708 only St. Augustine remained.[12] In Texas the missions failed not only because the Comanches and other nomadic tribes would not accept mission life but also because the Spaniards had to battle the French, who had expelled them from East Texas by 1719. The missioners also perished in Indian attacks. Yet, bigger losses were due to political changes.

In 1767 the Jesuits were expelled from the Spanish Empire. Caught in a struggle between the papacy and the Bourbon monarchs of Europe, the order had earlier been banned from Portugal and its colonies in 1759. Then it was dissolved by Pope Clement XIV in 1773 and not restored as a world order until 1814.[13] The missions principally affected in what is now the United States were those in Arizona, permanently established in 1731, two decades after Eusebio Kino's death. Chronologically, the second exodus occurred between 1793 and the 1830s, when the missions were secularized. The objective, to replace Franciscan missionaries with secular priests, was only partially achieved. Consequently, many of the missions were abandoned. The missions in California were ruined by secularization, which began in 1834. Under that process, administration was transferred from the Franciscans to secular clergy and the mission lands were parceled out to those who worked them, the Indians, but the mestizos and Spaniards ended up as the owners. The third big loss of mission personnel occurred after Mexico won its independence in 1821. Many of the clergy, being Spanish nationals, returned voluntarily to Spain. Others were expelled. Finally, on December 20, 1827, the Mexican government ordered the expulsion of Franciscans from New Mexico and Arizona, leaving many of the missions and settlements without priests.[14] All these developments slowly sapped the zeal of the missionaries.

The missionaries had also become lax in learning Indian languages. When he visited the missions in New Mexico in 1760, Bishop Tamaron criticized the failure to learn Indian languages. A report in 1776 showed the language deficiency was widespread.[15] By 1817 no missionaries in New Mexico spoke Indian languages.[16] In upper New Mexico the missions served an Indian population of twelve thousand in 1750; by 1800, the numbers had dropped to ten thousand and remained at that level. In Texas, most of the Indians had fled the missions by 1813.

Organization of the Church

In the Southwest and West, Franciscans headquartered in Mexico directed the missions (except in Arizona, administered by the Jesuits until 1767). The Colegio de La Santa Cruz de Queretaro, built in the 1680s, provided the missioners for Texas and later for Arizona; the Colegio de San Fernando el Grande for California and briefly for Texas; the Provincia del Santo Evangelio for El Paso and New Mexico; and the Colegio de Guadalupe de Zacatecas for Texas and later California. The

Franciscan colleges were founded to carry out the work of the Congregation of the Faith, created by Pope Gregory XV in 1622.

The northern colonial provinces were also under the jurisdiction of dioceses in Mexico. Initially, New Mexico was nominally under the Diocese of Guadalajara. After 1621 it became part of the newly created Diocese of Durango. The Diocese of Linares, created in 1777 and later renamed Monterey or Nuevo Leon, received jurisdiction over Texas, previously under the Diocese of Guadalajara. The Diocese of Sonora, whose first bishop arrived in 1783, included Arizona and California.

The bishops rarely visited their far-off provinces. A bishop trekked to New Mexico only three times during the eighteenth century.[17] During one period seventy years passed before a bishop came to visit. Yet in New Mexico the rarity of episcopal visits is not necessarily evidence of neglect, as charged by some historians, because from 1730 onward the bishop had a vicar representing him in Santa Fe. The closest New Mexico came to receiving adequate pastoral care was in the waning days of the Mexican period. Bishop José Antonio Laureano de Zubiría, ordained bishop of Durango in 1831, made three visits to New Mexico, in 1833, 1845, and 1850. After the first visit he bestowed on Father Juan Felipe Ortiz, a native New Mexican from Santa Fe, the power to administer the sacrament of confirmation. Padre Antonio José Martínez also received the authority to confirm. No bishop set foot in Texas or Arizona during the Mexican period: 1821–36 in Texas, 1821–46 in Arizona.

Until 1798 parishes headed by secular priests did not exist in New Mexico. In the Province of Texas two parishes were founded, in San Antonio and La Bahia, during the eighteenth century. In 1767 the bishop of Durango recommended that four of New Mexico's Franciscan posts be turned over to priests from the diocese: the Spanish towns of Santa Fe, Santa Cruz de La Cañada, Albuquerque, and El Paso.[18] The change was desirable, in the bishop's view, because colonists rather than Indians populated these settlements. The change, however, was delayed for decades.

The Franciscans, in a struggle for power, resisted the bishop's effort to extend his authority over the church in New Mexico. Nevertheless, by 1820 five secular priests served these towns. After Mexican independence officials in the Diocese of Durango ordered the secularization of five more missions. By 1840 the last of the Franciscan friars in New Mexico had died. A symbolic Franciscan presence returned when the bishop of Durango sent Fray Mariano de Jesús López in 1845. He served among the Zuni, Laguna, and Acoma Indians until his death in 1848. No other Franciscans joined him.[19] Secular clergy increased to eight in 1829 and to eleven in 1846.

In California there were no secular priests in 1840 and only five in 1846. Two secular priests served in Texas in 1836, and none in Arizona in 1846.[20] The Franciscans, dependent on Spain for vocations, had no local seminaries. More than 100 years elapsed after Juan de Oñate established the first missions before the area could claim its first priest. Santiago de Roybal, ordained about 1728 by the bishop of Durango, was the first native secular priest in the Southwest. Apparently, the Franciscans ordained no New Mexicans; Fray Angelico Chavez, a twentieth-century historian, claimed to be the first native Franciscan since the reconquest of New Mexico in 1693.[21]

Nevertheless, vocations were there, awaiting a man of vision to develop them. When Bishop José Antonio Laureano de Zubiría made his first visit to New Mexico in 1833, a priest named Antonio José Martínez offered to establish a preparatory school for seminarians. With Zubiría's blessing, thirty students studied at the school and sixteen were eventually ordained to the priesthood, most of them by Bishop Zubiría and four by French Bishop Jean Lamy, the first prelate of the Diocese of New Mexico,[22] who arrived in 1850. A few native vocations to the priesthood also developed in Texas in the 1790s and 1800s. Unfortunately, New Mexico had fewer than fifteen years to develop its own clergy. Lamy and his successors preferred to look for priestly vocations in Europe, particularly France. Bishops in other parts of the Southwest followed the same pattern.

For two hundred years Rome refused to establish dioceses in the Southwest. In 1630 Fray Alonso de Benavides had asked the pope to establish one in New Mexico. The next requests, also in vain, came from the Spanish Cortes in 1818, and from the Mexican Congress in 1823 and again in 1830. Finally, in 1840, responding to another request from the Mexican government, the Vatican established a diocese encompassing upper and lower California. The bishop, Francisco García Diego y Moreno, was consecrated the same year but did not arrive in Santa Barbara, the seat of the new diocese, until the end of 1841. Difficulties in recruiting clergy in Mexico prevented him from organizing the diocese well; there were only seventeen Franciscans in upper California. He did recruit seminarians in Mexico and ordained six of them during his six-year tenure. Already fifty-five when he became bishop, he died in 1846, the year the United States seized the Southwest from Mexico.

In New Mexico and Texas dioceses were established only after Mexico had lost those territories. Three years after Texas won its independence, the pope severed that territory from its Mexican diocese, made it a prefecture, and named Frenchman John L. Odin vice-prefect apostolic. In 1842 Odin was consecrated bishop, and in 1847 Texas became a diocese.

The Church of the Poor

Looking back, historians saw Spanish efforts to evangelize the indigenous people of lands now in the United States as a glorious period. It was carried out at enormous cost in resources, dedication, privation, and sacrifice. Between 1542 and 1834, on lands colonized or explored by the Spaniards, eighty-seven men gave up their lives as martyrs.[23] The Catholic faith took root everywhere and survived in spite of the constant conflict between Europeans and Indians and among the colonizing European powers. But the faith that flourished was an alloy of the beliefs of the missioners and those of the indigenous people, just as the people who survived and thrived blended the blood of the Indian and the Spaniard. The two cultures created not only a new people but also a new religion, one with the essentials of Catholicism but also with the spirit and some of the religious traditions of the indigenous peoples. Therefore, in counting martyrs, the toll among Indians who died for their religious beliefs has to be taken into account, to be sure, a count that will never be known but one many times greater than that of the Spanish missionaries.

By 1800 in New Mexico the settlements of mestizos had increased to 102. Villages and towns had also been built in Texas along the Rio Grande and in the area of present-day San Antonio, as well as in Arizona and in California. These people, viewed as inferior by the Creoles (Spaniards born in the New World) and as a "mongrel race" by Americans who conquered the region beginning with the Texas revolution in 1836, constituted the church of the poor. They flourished amid extremes of climate, attacks by hostile tribes, and the struggle demanded by a harsh land. Hardly literate peasants, served only by a few priests, at first lacking dioceses and even parishes, these people developed a self-reliant religion that endured. It is to them that the faith owes its existence in the Southwest.

The religiosity of the mestizos teemed with the "spiritual and material images of their crucified Nazarene and the queenly virgin."[24] They were inclined to strong penances, a legacy both of the Spaniards—Juan de Oñate scourged himself—and of their Indian ancestors. In New Mexico the colonists organized the Fraternidad Piadosa de Nuestro Padre Jesús Nazareno, commonly known as the Penitentes. The origin of the group is unknown, though some scholars link it to the Third Order of St. Francis, a lay branch of the Franciscans in existence during the Spanish period.

The Penitentes led their communities in the observance of the feasts of the liturgical calendar. For Lent and Holy Week they had elaborate penitential rituals, reenacting the crucifixion and leading the congregation in the Rosary and in reciting the Stations of the Cross. When someone died, they presided over the burial. They also taught Christian doctrine to the young, provided material assistance to those in need, and mediated disputes among families. "It would not be an exaggeration to say that these Penitentes assured the survival of the Catholic Faith in New Mexico during the Mexican period and beyond," wrote the priest who was chaplain of the Penitentes in 1988.[25]

Bishop Zubiria judged the penitential practices of the Penitentes as excessive. His successors tried to control their devotions; failing, they denied sacraments or ministry to its members. But since they had the support of the people, the Penitentes endured. There was a partial restoration in 1947. Archbishop Edwin V. Byrne formally recognized "the Brothers of Jesus of Nazareth (commonly called the Penitentes) as a pious Catholic society and agreed to guide the Brotherhood himself."[26] But not until 1974, when Roberto Sanchez was ordained the first native Hispanic archbishop of the Archdiocese of Santa Fe, were the Penitentes fully reconciled. Yet tensions still existed at the beginning of the twenty-first century.

To this day in the remote villages of New Mexico, still visited only rarely by clergy, the faith of the people reveals the self-reliance, strong religious life, and devotion built by the Penitentes.

Part III

American Conquest and the Melting-Pot Church

Chapter 3

A New Conquest
(1848–1890)

Early in the nineteenth century a new conquest started in the Southwest. North American trappers and traders began to enter New Mexico. Clipper ships began to visit ports in California. Settlers began moving into Texas. Under the Spanish policy of closed borders these visitors were seen as interlopers and expelled. But when Mexico won its independence, they were welcomed. The Mexican government gave Stephen Austin and three hundred North American families a grant in Texas. In New Mexico some trappers bought large tracts of land, a policy criticized by Father Antonio José Martínez. He also denounced the exploitation of the Indians by the North Americans.[1] North Americans also settled in California, marrying the daughters of some of the leading citizens. These settlers turned out to be the vanguard of an invasion.

In the mid-1830s the North American settlers in Texas revolted. By 1836 they had defeated Mexico's army and proclaimed their independence. In the meantime, Anglo Americans in other parts of the Southwest were helping to condition public opinion in the United States to seize the rest of those territories. They sent back highly unfavorable reports about the Hispanic inhabitants of the Southwest.

The cause of the conflict was "lust for seizure."[2] The administration of President James A. Polk decided to annex California.

First Polk tried to bribe Mexican officials; then he tried to start a revolution. Next he attempted to compel Mexico to sell California. When all that failed, the United States declared war. The purpose of the invasion was not only to seize the coveted territory but to humiliate Mexico. One army marched through New Mexico, Arizona, and California. Another crossed the Rio Grande at Matamoros, Eagle Pass, and El Paso. Ultimately, a third one landed at Vera Cruz and, following the invasion route of Hernán Cortez, captured Mexico City in 1847.

The invaders committed many crimes. Some of the soldiers raped mothers and daughters in the presence of their husbands and fathers.[3] They also desecrated churches. General Zachary Taylor, commanding one of the armies, collected $1 million from the Mexican people by force of arms. As a consequence of such acts, bitterness endured for generations.

The United States annexed half of Mexico's territory, including Texas, whose independence had not been recognized by Mexico but which the United States had admitted as a state in 1845. These territories contained, in addition to 180,000 to 250,000 Indians, between 75,000 and 100,000 inhabitants with at least partial Hispanic heritage. Most of them, about 60,000, lived in New Mexico. Of the remainder, about 8,000 lived in California, 2,000 in Arizona, and the rest in Texas. Through the Treaty of Guadalupe Hidalgo, signed in 1848, they became citizens of the United States, with specific guarantees of their civil rights and land titles. It soon became evident, however, that the provisions of the treaty would not be honored.

Anglo Americans refused to accept the Hispanics as equals. Many agreed with the political philosopher John C. Calhoun that only the "free white race" should be added to the union.[4]

Many also agreed with Anglo Americans in California who were willing to allow nonwhites to live there, "but only if they had few or no human rights and if they could be considered without argument to be born inferior."[5] As a result of these views, Hispanics suffered violence whose exact toll will never be known. But between 1865 and 1920, according to estimates, more Mexicans were lynched in the Southwest than blacks in the Old South.[6]

The violence was so intense and widespread in some areas that it gave the impression that the white race was crushing out the inferior race and that the Mexicans were doomed. In California two thousand miners attacked a foothills town inhabited by Mexicans, Chileans, and Peruvians, killing scores. Elsewhere, people were hanged on the basis of unsubstantiated accusations or for misdemeanors. A man was lynched for getting into a fistfight, a woman for killing a miner who broke into her house, a man for refusing to play the fiddle for a group of Anglo Texans.

Historian Walter Prescott Webb wrote that one law applied to Mexicans and another, less rigorous, to political leaders and prominent Americans.[7] In West Texas, Judge Roy Bean could find nothing in the law that made killing a Mexican a crime. Writing about that period, novelist James Michener reported that "Anglo children who once had been taught that Indians were not human were now raised to think that Mexicans were even less so."[8]

Besides physical violence, Hispanics suffered what later came to be called institutional violence. In the courts they were sometimes disqualified from being witnesses because they were not white. Through legal and illegal means they were denied the right to vote. Squatters who seized their lands were not prosecuted; neither were persons who assaulted them. But if the victims defended themselves, they were punished severely. Real-estate taxes were raised until Hispanic owners lost their properties for being delinquent; then the rates were lowered for the new Anglo American owners. Other Hispanics were dispossessed by means of a statute that required validation of all land titles issued by Mexico. In California a "foreign miners' tax" was imposed on Hispanics who had become citizens through the Treaty of Guadalupe Hidalgo. As time passed, Hispanics were excluded from all but menial jobs, receiving no opportunity to develop new skills.

In economic terms the effect of the physical and institutional violence was to impoverish Hispanics as a people. During colonial and Mexican times society had consisted of a small upper class of those in top government positions, officers in the army, ranchers, and large landowners. Beneath them were the majority of the settlers—artisans, cowboys and foremen on the ranches, and craftsmen and tradesmen in the settlements. The Indians were the lowest class of workers.[9] The Anglo American conquest reduced many to the lowest level. Only where Hispanic Americans were the majority, or a high proportion of the population, as in New Mexico, El Paso, and San Antonio, were they able to retain strong political and economic influence. Whereas Hispanics as a people once owned countless horses, vast herds of sheep, and lands stretching to distant horizons, within two or three decades they found themselves on reduced acreage or holding only the poorest lands. Judge Don Pablo de la Guerra, one of the authors of the California Constitution, said in a speech before the legislature: "I have seen old men of sixty and seventy years of age weeping because they have been cast out of their ancestral home. They have been humiliated and insulted. They have been refused the privilege of cutting their own firewood."[10]

As another effect of the conquest, Hispanics were branded a criminal population. Since the authorities would not protect them, they had to take the law into their own hands when attacked or dispossessed. They were then hunted down as bandits. In fact, many of these guerrilla fighters were taking the only option available to them. Tiburcio Vasquez, one of those caught and hanged, said he had only tried to avenge Yankee injustices committed against his people: "I believe we were being unjustly deprived of the social rights that belonged to us."[11] Today, historians and sociologists, both Anglo and Hispano, are likely to see these incidents of "banditry" as justified retaliation rather than crime.[12]

Violence and discrimination forced many ordinary people as well as leaders to emigrate, usually to Mexico. One of the heroes of the Texas Revolution, Captain Juan Seguin, later the mayor of San Antonio, was one of those exiles. "I had to leave Texas, abandon all, for which I had fought and spent my fortune, to become a wanderer."[13]

The worst effect, however, was a complex of defeatism, apparent indifference, passivity, and lack of motivation that continued to affect many Hispanics into the twentieth century. The people felt that no matter what they did, they would remain on the periphery of the economic, political, and social systems.

The absolute subjugation of the Hispanic population became possible because Anglo Americans controlled the armed forces, the police, the courts, the legislatures, and the economy. The discovery of gold in California nine days after the signing of the Treaty of Guadalupe Hidalgo in 1848 brought so many settlers that in a year they outnumbered the Mexicans ten to one. By 1850 California had 380,000 inhabitants, only 15 percent of them Hispanics, and the proportion continued to decline. Between 1851 and 1860, only 4,302 Hispanics entered the state. By 1870 those of Spanish origin accounted for only 4 percent of the population. Between 1851 and 1900 they were less than 1 percent of the immigrants to California.[14] Low immigration was due to the extreme violence and discrimination that Hispanics experienced in California during that period. In Texas, Anglo Americans moved in so fast during the 1820s and 1830s that by 1836, when the territory declared itself a republic, they numbered 30,000, with only 5,000 Mexicans. In 1846 the population had gone up to 140,000, with very little of that increase consisting of Hispanics.[15] Only in New Mexico did the Hispanics remain in the majority until the twentieth century.

Beginning in the 1880s Hispanics in the Southwest obtained a reprieve from the categorical rejection they had suffered in most areas since 1846. Now they were welcomed and even recruited—but only as cheap labor in a few industries, among them agriculture, the railroads, and mining. Workers were recruited not only in the Mexican American barrios but also in Mexico itself. The new policy could be traced to a number of developments. In 1882 Congress passed the Chinese Exclusion Act, which halted emigration from China to the United States. A few years later a similar agreement curtailed immigration of Japanese. In the 1920s new laws excluded Eastern Europeans. As a result, Mexicans and Mexican Americans were in great demand for menial labor. They were chosen because they were docile, hardworking, and easy to "send home" when they were no longer needed. They were simply transported to the Mexican border.

At the same time, irrigation opened millions of acres for growing fruits and vegetables. The completion of the first transcontinental railroad in 1869 and the development of refrigerated railroad cars in 1887 made it possible to ship produce to the populated centers of the East. Passage of a tariff on the importation of sugar facilitated the growth of the sugar-beet industry, which required much hand labor.

Thus Hispanics were finally assigned a place in Anglo American society, even if only a temporary and provisional one. They were welcome only if and when the labor for which they were designated was available. They were not considered equals to Anglo Americans, not welcome to associate socially with them, and not permitted to advance economically, politically, and socially.

Foreign Shepherds

Before the Mexican War only one diocese and one vicariate had headquarters in the Southwest. The Diocese of Upper and Lower California had been established in 1840, but the first bishop had not arrived until 1841. The same year Texas had been made a missionary vicariate subject to Rome. Dioceses were created rapidly following the change in sovereignty from Mexico to the United States. The Diocese of Galveston (Texas) was created in 1847; Santa Fe (New Mexico) in 1853; San Francisco in 1853; Sacramento (Grass Valley) in 1868;

San Antonio in 1874; Denver in 1887; Dallas in 1890; and Tucson in 1897.

With two exceptions, the first bishops of the dioceses in New Mexico, Arizona, Colorado, and Texas were French. The first prelate of San Antonio was an American of Minorcan (Spanish) descent, and the first in Dallas was Irish, Thomas Brennan. The first bishops of the dioceses of San Francisco and Los Angeles were Spanish, but an Irishman, Bishop Eugene O'Connell, was chosen for Sacramento. The Vicariate Apostolic of Brownsville was created in 1874 with another American of Minorcan descent as bishop.

These bishops, all but one born in Europe, attempted to create a church like the one they had left. The one who perhaps tried the hardest was Jean Baptiste Lamy, the first bishop of New Mexico. He boasted that he was creating a little Auvergne, the name of his province in France. Even the architectural style of the cathedral he started in Santa Fe was French, as were the artisans he brought in to build it.

Lamy was particularly concerned with ecclesiastical buildings: churches, chapels, schools, and hospitals. He was successful. Fifteen years after his arrival, he reported to the Holy See that he had built forty-five churches and chapels and had repaired eighteen or twenty old ones. Moreover, he had established four houses of the Sisters of Loretto and three of Christian Brothers. Lamy also established a seminary, but it lasted only a few years. Nevertheless, native New Mexicans who studied there were eventually ordained: José Samuel Garcia and Manuel Ribera. Lamy ordained four other natives between 1856 and 1859: Ramón Medina, Miguel Vigil, Manuel Chavez, and Sembran Tafoya.[16] But in general he preferred to staff the diocese and later archdiocese with Frenchmen. He or his associates made several trips to Europe to recruit both priests and brothers, and to Kentucky and Ohio to recruit sisters.

Lamy and his associate, Joseph P. Machebeuf, later the first bishop of Denver, have been credited with bringing Gallic discipline to the church in New Mexico. But he also caused a division that took generations to reconcile. The Council of Baltimore had appointed Lamy to head the Vicariate of New Mexico in *partibus infidelium* (in the region of the infidels), a fixed phrase for any missionary territory. The designation was perhaps justified in Texas, considering how many indigenous peoples were not yet converted. But it was clearly an affront to the Catholicism that had existed in New Mexico for 250 years. The biased view of the American church and of the bishops sent to the Southwest was that there had been a glorious period of evangelization by the missionaries from Spain and an almost total collapse of the church during the Mexican period. Perhaps that explains why Lamy's relations with the native clergy were poor. At one point he expressed the intent "to keep them under fear," and on one occasion he wrote to the bishop of Cincinnati: "I must be patient and catch them doing wrong. I suspended one of the senior clerics; perhaps that will be an example for the others."[17] Perhaps his hostility was due in part to the unceremonious reception he received when he arrived in Santa Fe. Not having received notification of the creation of the vicariate and the appointment of Lamy, the New Mexican clergy would not accept him without credentials signed by their bishop. They suggested he see Bishop Zubiria in Durango. Lamy therefore had to journey eight hundred miles on horseback to get the necessary papers.

There were sixteen priests in the Vicariate of New Mexico when Lamy arrived, but seven of them were old and sickly. Of the nine remaining, Lamy removed five, including the ones most respected by the people. The most famous was Antonio José Martínez, the pastor of Taos, who had been most responsible for building a native clergy. By failing to develop an effective seminary and relying so heavily on European clergy and religious, Lamy killed the tradition of priesthood that had begun to develop during the Mexican period. It would be generations and five French bishops later before an Anglo American bishop would try to revive it.

Texas

Though the first bishops in Texas were also French, the church they encountered was different from that of New Mexico in one significant respect. In New Mexico the majority of the inhabitants were Hispanics and would remain so until the middle of the twentieth century. But in Texas, Mexican Americans were a minority of the population. Immigrants were arriving so fast from Germany, Czechoslovakia, France, and Poland that Father John Timon, who was named prefect apostolic of Texas in 1839, could entertain the notion that these immigrants would be the primary flock. At least a few priests preferred to serve the immigrants rather than the Mexicans. Father Florent Vandenberghe tried to persuade the Jesuits to take responsibility for Brownsville so that he could work among "civilized people" in Louisiana or North Texas.[18] When Father Dominic Manucy was appointed to head the new Vicariate Apostolic of Brownsville, he responded with a letter saying: "I consider this appointment as Vicar Apostolic of Brownsville the worst sentence that could have been given me for any crime. The Catholic population is composed almost exclusively of Mexican greasers—cattle drovers and thieves. No money can be got out of these people, not even to bury their fathers."[19]

The attitudes of Jean M. Odin, the first bishop of the Diocese of Galveston (encompassing all of Texas), toward Mexicans are not clear. He made great efforts to recruit priests in Europe for European immigrants. He also brought three Spaniards to work along the San Antonio River and left them there throughout the 1840s. Then, and subsequently in some areas, classes were taught in Spanish, and foreign clergy learned Spanish instead of English and served Hispanics all their lives. But in 1840 he removed the only two native priests above the Nueces Valley. As one of the French priests put it bluntly, the way to make progress was to replace the Mexican clergy with foreigners.[20]

The issue was not so much ministry as it was who was to provide it. There the early bishops of Texas showed a decided preference for Europeans over natives.

The bishops of Texas built institutions, but the work was slow. In 1849 there were only twelve priests in all of Texas to serve twenty thousand Catholics. By 1860 there were only forty-two churches and forty-four chapels in the state—hardly adequate for the burgeoning population. In rural areas four priests served eighty thousand people. Like Lamy, the French bishops recruited religious congregations and orders to come to Texas: the Oblates of Mary Immaculate, the Sisters of the Incarnate Word, and other groups from Europe. But though each of the sisters' congregations found several native vocations, the clergy did not find candidates for the priesthood. The progress reports tell of the completion of churches, chapels, schools, colleges, and hospitals, but not seminaries. They could not seem to get them off the ground. Mexico could not have provided any priests if the Texas bishops requested them; many Spaniards had returned home when Mexico won its independence. But when twenty-two Sisters of Charity who had been forced to leave Mexico because of church-state conflicts at the time[21] arrived in Brownsville in 1875, Manucy refused to accept them. Like Lamy, the bishops of Texas went to Europe again and again to find most of their clergy and religious.

Some clergy thought the primary beneficiaries of these church institutions and of the clergy and religious brought from Europe ought to be the dominant English-speaking population. For example, an Oblate priest in Brownsville thought St. Joseph College should cater to the governing class.[22] Due to lack of resources, not goodwill, the Sisters of Charity of the Incarnate Word in their early years in Texas concentrated their efforts on non-Hispanic people. Schools they opened for Mexican American children often had to be closed. The Sisters of the Incarnate Word and Blessed Sacrament, however, established themselves first in the heavily Hispanic settlements of Brownsville and Corpus Christi.

In Texas and New Mexico the European clergy did not understand some aspects of Hispanic piety. Father Timon marveled at how Hispanics were ready to die for their religion but hardly knew what it was about. In the wake of Protestant challenge, knowledge of the faith had become of paramount importance. But for heirs of an austere Iberian spirituality who had experienced neither the Protestant Reformation nor the Catholic Counter-Reformation, it was not what one knew but how one lived that made all the difference.

California

When Bishop Diego y Moreno died in 1846, the embryonic institutional Mexican American church began to die as well. He had established Our Lady of Guadalupe Seminary, near Santa Ines Mission, in 1844. By the end of the following year it had thirty-three students, though only a few were considered serious candidates for the priesthood. The seminary made it a policy to admit as many poor students as its resources would permit. After the bishop died, the seminary could not get the support it needed, and though it continued for seventeen years, apparently no native Mexican American priests were ordained. Almost a century would pass in southern California before there would be another diocesan seminary, St. John Seminary, founded in 1939 in Camarillo. Things moved faster in the north, where Hispanics were a tiny minority; St. Patrick Seminary was established in Menlo Park in 1898. The Catholic Church as institution grew rapidly in the years following Anglo American occupation. In 1851 a newspaper article boasted that "in almost every portion of the state, churches are erected, charitable and literary institutions are being founded and with the blessing of God we hope in a short time that California will shine forth a bright spot on the map of the Catholic Church."[23] As previously mentioned, the first see, the Diocese of Monterey, had split in two by the early 1850s, creating the

Archdiocese of San Francisco. In the 1860s the Diocese of Grass Valley, later changed to Sacramento, was established.

Before he died Bishop García Diego y Moreno named a fellow Franciscan, Father José Gonzáles Rubio, a Mexican, as his vicar general. Rubio guided the far-flung diocese until 1850, when a Spanish Dominican, Joseph Sadoc Alemany, was appointed bishop. In 1853 Alemany was promoted to head the new Archdiocese of San Francisco; Thaddeus Amat, another Spaniard, succeeded him at Monterey. But in less than fifty years the bishops of California would all be Irish. The first was the aforementioned Eugene O'Connell, the first bishop of Sacramento, who was succeeded by another Irishman, Patrick Manogue, in 1884. Alemany, who served in San Francisco until 1884, was followed by Archbishop Patrick Riordan. Amat, who died in 1878, was succeeded by another Spaniard, Bishop Francis Mora. But when he resigned in 1896, Bishop George Montgomery took over. Irish domination of the California hierarchy was now complete.

California had only sixteen priests (eleven Franciscans and five secular clergy) when it was occupied by the United States. When Father Gonzáles Rubio saw the tide of immigrants arrive following the discovery of gold, he recruited priests in France and Oregon. Thanks to the generous response he received, especially from Oregon Archbishop Norbert Blanchet, he had twenty-eight priests when Alemany arrived a few years later. Alemany, who heard the news of his appointment while attending a general chapter of his order in Rome, recruited more priests in France, England, Ireland, and brought one from Spain.

The best response to these recruiting efforts came from Ireland. According to the San Francisco Archdiocesan Directory, of the 231 priests who served there from 1848 to 1904, 146 (63.2 percent) were trained in Ireland. Only four priests, less than 2 percent, were trained in Spain, and none was trained in Mexico. A survey of the religious orders showed the same pattern.[24]

In contrast to the growth of Irish clergy, the number of Hispanic priests steadily declined. When Alemany arrived, there were eleven Mexican priests in California. By 1856 there were four fewer; two had died, and the other two had returned to Mexico.

The Christian Experience of the Poor

Alemany, who was generally well disposed toward the Mexicans, was concerned about the lack of Hispanic priests. He therefore asked for and received permission to establish a Franciscan novitiate and seminary, the Apostolic College of Our Lady of Sorrows. But Amat did not share his countryman's sympathies. He became embroiled in a dispute with the Franciscans and tried to force them to leave the college and minister to Indians at Mission San Luis Rey. Rome eventually ruled in favor of the Franciscans, but then Amat canceled their faculties. Though they were restored three years later, the college languished until it was closed in 1900.

Throughout this period Hispanic influence steadily declined. Archbishop John Hughes of New York took the trouble to write to José de La Guerra, a leading Catholic layman in California, to ask him about the condition of the church. The Californian urged that a Hispanic be named to head it and added, "I think that at least it is indispensable that the bishop or bishops who are appointed be proficient in Spanish."[25] Alemany seemed to have the same concern, for he appointed Gonzáles Rubio as his vicar. While Alemany was the bishop of Monterey, there was more sensitivity to the multicultural nature of the California church. For example, one of eighteen decrees approved by an assembly of the clergy said that couples getting married had a right to choose a priest from their own ethnic group to officiate at the ceremony.

Amat, however, was much less sympathetic to the Hispanics. In addition to his dispute with the Franciscans—or perhaps because of it—he removed Gonzáles Rubio from his post as vicar general. The priest spent his remaining years, until his death in 1875, trying to save the Franciscan novitiate.

As Hispanics became a smaller proportion of the population in Texas and California, their culture and traditions as well as their persons came under increasing attack. In Arizona in the 1890s, for example, some municipalities passed ordinances banning Mexican fiestas. Amat published a pastoral letter critical of Mexican American religious practices. The bishop, historian Michael Neri judged later, was afraid that the public processions and private devotions of the Hispanics would stir anti-Catholic feelings among the Protestants.[26] This same concern caused, at least in part, the continuing dispute with the Penitentes in New Mexico, whose activities were considered "contrary to modern ecclesiastical order and harmful to the image of Catholicism in the eyes of newcomers from the East."[27] Lamy found support for his desire to ban some of their practices in the "outspoken hostility of anti-Catholic civil leaders in the territory."[28]

Lamy tried without success to impose the rules of the Third Order of St. Francis on the Penitentes. Then he started a policy of verifying, during administration of the sacraments, whether the recipient was a Penitente. If he was and refused to renounce membership, he was denied the sacrament. Lamy's directive was not carried out by some of the priests. When the bishop went on to deny the Penitentes the status of a religious society, they were incorporated as a benevolent society by the territorial legislature.

Jean Baptist Salpointe, who succeeded Lamy, made further efforts to ban the Penitentes. He ordered pastors to deny the sacraments to those who insisted on observing traditional wakes. The order could not be enforced in isolated villages without priests. Even in the twentieth century, when a person died in the rural areas, the Penitentes had to lead the wake, dig the grave, and conduct the burial service. Many priests, therefore, did not enforce the rule. The Jesuits, in particular, did not cooperate, and for that reason Salpointe forced them to leave New Mexico.[29]

The Penitentes in New Mexico represented what today would be called a parallel church that operated in rural areas where the official church had limited contact. Though their secrecy (another of the objections raised against them) and their penances may have seemed excessive to the newcomers from the East, the Penitentes provided structure to the church where there was no clergy. Yet the ecclesial authorities caused unnecessary alienation by trying to ban the brotherhood. Fortunately, most people still filled the churches and chapels when priests were available and, at the same time, continued their traditional religious practices. Some people simply limited their contact with the church to those occasions that were absolutely essential: baptisms, marriages, and funerals. In Taos and in the San Luis Valley in Colorado, Presbyterians gained many converts. One historian wrote: "Many Penitentes, feeling rejected by the church of their forebears, converted to Presbyterianism. Some went on to become lay or ordained ministers."[30] Alienation was also caused by failure of the bishops and clergy to defend Hispanics. During this era there was much violence against Hispanics; lynchings for little or no reason were common throughout the Southwest. If bishops and clergy spoke out in defense of the victims, no record was kept. More likely, they remained silent out of desire to be accepted by secular society. This was not an era when the church distinguished itself in its defense of the oppressed.

As in civil society, a process of conquest occurred in the church. The new leaders imposed their authority by displacing the previous leaders of the community. In New Mexico, Lamy excommunicated the most brilliant pastor: Padre Antonio José Martínez. Born in 1793 in Abiquiu, Martínez was a descendant of one of the settlers who had come with Juan de Oñate in 1598. He was married at the age of nineteen, but his wife died a year later in childbirth. The child, a daughter, survived only until the age of twelve. Four years after he became a widower, at the age of twenty-four, Martínez entered the seminary in Durango. He was ordained on February 10, 1822, at the age of twenty-nine, by Bishop Juan Francisco de Castanizo. He returned to New Mexico in 1823 and served at Tome Pueblo and later at Taos, where he became the pastor in 1826.

Martínez distinguished himself not just by his efforts "to become a true minister of Christ,"[31] but by his interest in education. He started a coeducational school, an idea unheard-of at that time, and also a school to train seminarians. Among the many young men he propelled toward the priesthood was another talented New Mexican who was removed by Lamy, José Manuel Gallegos. In 1846, when the United States seized the territory, Martínez was fifty-three years old.

Martínez served as a member of the New Mexico legislature during the Mexican period and also during the early years of the North American administration. His involvement in politics, however, went much deeper. In 1847, when Indians and Hispanics revolted in Taos and killed the American governor, the plan was reportedly made in the home of Vicar Juan Felipe Ortiz, with Martínez and another priest in attendance. The revolt was crushed and Martínez's alleged complicity was never proved. Nevertheless, he was the man the North Americans feared most.

When Martínez was sixty-four years old, Lamy excommunicated him "for grave and scandalous faults, his writings against due order and discipline in the Church."[32] The immediate cause of his expulsion was Martínez's opposition to the collection of tithes, as demanded by the bishop. But beneath the surface was a conflict that has occurred again and again between Hispanics and their European and North American bishops. In one sense it is based on differences in piety and culture; in another, it is a struggle for self-determination by a people who have had only a peripheral role in the church since 1850.

Martínez refused to obey the excommunication order and continued to serve as a priest and to celebrate Mass in his private chapel for a few followers. Gallegos was removed from San Felipe Parish in Albuquerque. Lamy accused him of being absent without leave from his parish and of living scandalously. The real reason, a New Mexico priest believed, was that the new French leadership wanted control of the most prosperous parishes.[33] After his suspension, Gallegos, who was respected by the people, was elected a territorial delegate to Congress. Vicar Ortiz was also removed and replaced with a Frenchman.

Though some prominent laymen supported the French bishop, others opposed him. One sent a petition to Rome asking that Lamy be removed and replaced with Martínez. The Frenchmen, however, could do little about laymen directing religious ceremonies in remote villages without their knowledge and permission. They were never numerous enough or powerful enough to stop the Penitentes.

The political involvement of the church of the poor was not just confined to the actions of certain priests. The Penitentes dominated politics throughout northern New Mexico and areas of southern Colorado inhabited by Hispanics. The church authorities condemned such political involvement but could do little to stop it. At the edge of those same Penitente strongholds during the last part of the nineteenth century a secret society called the Gorras Blancas waged war against the ranchers who had acquired large landholdings by questionable means. Their platform was to protect the rights and interests of the people in general and especially those of the helpless classes. The church that Lamy created had no contact with, control over, or sympathy for these fighters for justice.

By the end of the nineteenth century Hispanic Americans in the Southwest had no institutional voice in the church. The native Hispanic priests who had been their spokesmen in mid-century had all been purged or died out. The removal of the activists had been a powerful lesson for those aging priests who remained. They had realized that they could remain only if they were submissive. They had faded away quietly.

The Hispanic laity, assumed to be inferior to the Anglo Americans and immigrants from Europe, simply returned to their old ways. For almost three hundred years in New Mexico, two hundred years in Texas, and one hundred years in California, they relied, of necessity, on their own homespun religious traditions. These served them well.

Due to violence and lack of economic opportunity, Hispanic immigration to the Southwest was minimal during the latter part of the nineteenth century except perhaps in south Texas. At the same time, however, Hispanics were beginning to establish themselves in the Southeast. As Cubans struggled for their independence during the last half of the century, exiles began to settle in Tampa, Florida. After Cuba's independence following the Spanish American War in 1898, the continued political turmoil stimulated ongoing migration to the United States.

On July 25, 1898, United States troops invaded Puerto Rico. The Treaty of Paris ending the war made Puerto Rico a possession of the United States. During the nineteenth century the population had increased from 150,000 to nearly one million.[34] The economic policies of the Island's new rulers would create the conditions for a future mass migration to the mainland. Since Puerto Rico had been coveted to develop sugar production, North Americans soon acquired huge tracts of land for plantations.

The dispossessed peasants moved to the cities, increasing unemployment.

Chapter 4

Growth and Conflict
(1890–1946)

Although in absolute numbers the Hispanic population increased in the last half of the nineteenth century, it had declined steadily as a proportion of the total population throughout the Southwest. This trend lent authority to the hypothesis that the Hispanic, like the Indian, was destined to disappear. The church, accepting that view, acted accordingly. It gave first priority to the Anglo Americans and the immigrants from Europe. The bishops and clergy did serve the Hispanic people but seemed to view such work as temporary. That is the inescapable conclusion of statements of the early French clergy in Texas expressing satisfaction at Mexican emigration from Texas.

About the turn of the century, however, a new awareness began to grow. It was as if, however dimly, the bishops and clergy realized that Hispanics were in the Southwest to stay and perhaps even to grow. Church leaders saw that the Spanish-speaking people were not only beginning to grow as a percentage of the total population but also spreading to other parts of the country. At that time the bishops, pastors, and religious congregations began to confront the challenge seriously. Nevertheless, such ministry was, in many cases, supplemental to the main responsibility of serving the dominant society. Limits were placed on Hispanic ministry so as not to offend Anglos. As late as 1940 Mexican religious practices that might be offensive to Anglo Americans were not permitted. Charles Buddy, the first bishop of San Diego, wrote that some practices were "a source of scandal and could easily weaken the faith of the people." He referred to dances held for the feast of Our Lady of Guadalupe and during processions of the Blessed Sacrament. Buddy canceled some of these celebrations.[1]

Texas

In Texas Spanish-surnamed clergy began to appear. Spanish Claretians established missions in the region around the turn of the century, Spanish Oblates of Mary Immaculate in the 1920s. Moreover, the religious orders and congregations of religious women, which in the past had seen their primary mission as serving the new immigrants from Germany or France, now began to devote at least part of their ministry to Hispanics. The Sisters of the Incarnate Word and Blessed Sacrament, for example, took over a hospital in Brownsville that served mostly Mexican Americans. In Fort Worth, St. Paul Hospital started a free clinic in the Mexican section of town in the 1920s. In 1907 the Sisters of Mercy began opening schools throughout the Rio Grande Valley.

For the first time, Mexican sisters started working in the Southwest. Shortly after the outbreak of the Mexican Revolution in 1910, the Society of Santa Teresa de Jesús took charge of a new parish school at Our Lady of Guadalupe Parish and also at San Felipe parishes in San Antonio and in Uvalde. Driven north by the Mexican Revolution and by the religious persecution that followed, other nuns and priests came to serve the Mexicans in the United States. Five Sisters of Charity fleeing Mexico in 1927 opened a convent in El Paso. Soon joined by eighteen others, they founded a home for delinquent girls.

At the same time, spiritual ministry to Hispanics improved. Bishop Pedro Verdaguer, the apostolic vicar of Brownsville, increased the number of Spanish-speaking clergy even though he had a low opinion of the Mexican people. He said they were unindustrious and superstitious. Between 1911 and 1913 so-called Mexican churches were going up in many areas. In 1915 St. Joseph Parish, headed by two priests with Spanish surnames, was founded in Fort Worth to serve Spanish-speaking people. These were the beginnings of a separate church for Hispanics. In part, at least, this was the reaction to prejudice. Anglos were not willing to mix with the Mexicans, even in church.[2]

In many places there was one church for Mexican Americans and one for Anglos. In other places, where the Hispanics lived in segregated neighborhoods, the Mexican churches were needed simply because there would be no other place for them to worship. By 1918 eighty-two new churches had been built in the Archdiocese of San Antonio alone, many of them for the Hispanic community.

Reinforcing the idea of separate churches, the clergy encouraged the Mexicans and Mexican Americans to form their own church organizations. In many parishes, therefore, *cofradias*, *sociedades*, and *apostolados* were organized. Father Juan Maiztegui, CM, founded the Association of Our Lady of Guadalupe in 1911 in San Antonio. This society, reorganized in 1932 as the Guadalupanas, spread throughout the Southwest and became the main guardian of the culture and religious traditions of the Hispanic people.

Around that time Rome began to establish dioceses in areas with a proportionately high Hispanic population. In 1912 Corpus Christi was established, with Bishop Paul Nussbaum in charge. Though he had previously voiced prejudice against Hispanics, he doubled the number of parochial schools to eighteen before ill health forced him to resign seven years later. Next was the Diocese of El Paso, founded in 1914. A. J. Schuler, a Jesuit, became the first bishop. He, like his contemporaries, built many schools, parishes, orphanages, and a hospital. Amarillo became the seat of another diocese in 1927, and

R. A. Gerken the first bishop. A year later San Antonio became an archdiocese.

During this period and for decades hence, the church of the Southwest, pleading that it was overextended and lacked resources, dealt only with spiritual matters and devoted little effort to work for social justice. Nonetheless, there were the beginnings of the social commitment of the latter half of the twentieth century. In 1930 Father Charles Taylor gathered 450 farm workers in Crystal City, Texas, to discuss labor conditions and to demand labor agreements from the growers. Another priest called attention to the prejudice of Anglos, especially those from the northern part of the country, who saw Mexicans as a lower race and wanted nothing to do with them except to use them for manual labor.[3]

The bishops of Texas continued to depend on foreign clergy rather than develop local Hispanic vocations. But in 1942 a priest visiting St. Anthony Seminary called attention to six Mexican American seminarians studying there. He said they were the "future of the province."[4]

California

California's Irish bishops also built many institutions, but they were largely for mainstream Catholics. An exception was Archbishop John L. Cantwell of Los Angeles, who addressed some of the needs of Mexican Americans. He built clinics and, in the 1920s, spent more than half of the archdiocese's social welfare budget on them.[5] Father Patrick Browne of St. Boniface Parish in Anaheim set up four chapels to serve migrant workers during the same period. In Oakland, Father Charles Philipps of St. Mary's Parish served migrant workers. Other bishops and clergy, however, acted as if they were not aware that Hispanics were an ever-larger part of their flock.

Archbishop Edward Hanna, who headed the Archdiocese of San Francisco from 1915 to 1935, was openly hostile. On one occasion he wrote to the California congressional delegation asking that immigration from Mexico be limited. The Mexicans, he said, "drain our charities; they and their children become a large portion of our jail population, affect the health of our community, create a problem in our labor camps, require special attention in our schools and are of low mentality, diminish the percentage of our white population and remain foreign."[6]

Content with the steady arrival of priests from Ireland, the bishops made less of an effort than bishops in Texas to bring in Spanish-speaking priests or develop native vocations. Between 1848 and 1945 the Archdiocese of San Francisco had no Hispanic seminarians. Not one of its diocesan priests was trained in Mexico and, among those in religious orders, only one, a Jesuit, was from Spain.[7] In San Jose, which has always had a large Hispanic population, no Mexican or Mexican American served as a pastor between 1852 and 1962.[8] The Franciscans required their seminarians to study six years of German but apparently no Spanish.[9]

New Mexico

When the fourth archbishop of New Mexico, Peter Bourgade, a Frenchman, was consecrated in 1899, two sermons were preached—one in English and one in Spanish. Significantly, the latter was by a French priest, not a native Hispanic. That vignette accurately characterized the church in New Mexico at that time. The French and other foreign priests held the leadership posts. Hispanics were virtually if not totally absent from the clergy and religious congregations. On the other hand, they continued to be the overwhelming majority of the flock. In southern Arizona, where a similar situation prevailed, the bishops were French but the lay leaders were Mexican or Mexican American.[10] In Tucson, as in New Mexico, Mexican Americans were the majority of the population through the 1920s and

1930s. At that time there were six parishes in town, four for Spanish speakers and two for English speakers. As in other areas, there was great institutional growth during that period. Since the Hispanics were the majority, they were, at least in part, the beneficiaries of the schools, hospitals, orphanages, and other institutions constructed by various groups. Many congregations of religious women began their work at that time—the Sisters of St. Francis, the Dominicans from various foundations in Michigan, the Sisters of the Sorrowful Mother. After an absence of about seventy years, the Franciscans returned to serve in missions for the Navajo Indians. But in one area, that of native vocations, the church continued its benign neglect.

In Fray Angelico Chavez's history of the Archdiocese of Santa Fe from 1846 to 1946, all the early pastors he mentions have French or other non-Hispanic surnames. This situation continued until Franciscan Albert Daeger succeeded the fifth and last French bishop, John Baptist Pitaval, in 1919. At that time Fray Chavez first mentions an Hispanic priest: "In 1920, Father Antonio Perez, eased out by the friars from the Cathedral rectory where he had been an assistant, founded the parish of San José in Raton."[11] Daeger, however, moved slowly. He did not ordain anyone until 1929.

"After many years of no native clerical vocations," Chavez writes, "Archbishop Daeger ordained three New Mexicans from 1929 on: Fathers José A. García of Santa Fe, Juan T. Sanchez of Tomé and Philip J. Cassidy of Mora."[12] Daeger established a minor seminary in Las Vegas, but it did not last long. His successor, Bishop Gerken of the Amarillo Diocese, became archbishop after Daeger's death in 1932. In 1935 Gerken started another seminary in Albuquerque and recruited Mexican Americans so that "'they can go back to eat beans in the pueblo."[13] Gerken purchased buildings originally built for a Protestant school and reopened it as Lourdes School, a combination seminary and industrial trade school for boys. Nevertheless, only in the 1940s, a century after the visionary Padre Antonio José Martínez had shown that the region was ready to ordain its own clergy, was a determined effort made to recruit native Hispanic clergy in New Mexico. In the mid-1940s Archbishop Edwin Vincent Byrne, who had been the first bishop of Ponce, Puerto Rico, founded Immaculate Heart of Mary Seminary in Santa Fe; the seminary closed in 1997 for lack of vocations.

During the 1930s and 1940s, only two native Hispanic priests receive any mention in Chavez's history: J. T. Sanchez, who built a large new church in Clayton; and José A. García, who had been ordained by Daeger, started a parish at Chaperito in 1935, and then went on to serve as pastor to the historic church of St. Francis (which, after 150 years as a mission, had finally been canonically established as a parish). Under Archbishop Byrne, García became pastor of St. Ignatius Parish in Albuquerque and finally held the post of vicar general. "It was the first time that a native priest has held any position of note since Fr. Juan Felipe Ortiz was vicar general in 1846," Fray Chavez writes.[14]

Regional and National Structures

During this period the church began for the first time to establish regional and national structures for Spanish speakers. In 1923 an immigration office was established by the US bishops in El Paso. But the most significant developments came in the waning days of World War II. In 1944 Archbishop Robert E. Lucey of San Antonio sponsored a seminar for Spanish speakers. About fifty delegates from western and southwestern dioceses met for three days to discuss all aspects of the church's work with Hispanics. A second seminar was held the same year at the request of Archbishop Urban J. Vehr of Denver. Delegates from California, Arizona, New Mexico, Colorado, Wyoming, Oklahoma, and Texas attended.

As a result, many dioceses in the Far West and Southwest established Catholic councils for Spanish speakers; councils were later organized in dioceses of the Midwest and Northwest where migrants worked in the fields. In 1945 fourteen bishops organized the Bishops' Committee for the Spanish Speaking. With funds provided by the American Board of Catholic Missions, the committee's staff began an intensive program of social and spiritual aid in four provinces—Los Angeles, Santa Fe, Denver, and San Antonio. The first part of the program included construction of clinics, settlement houses, and community and catechetical centers; the second, services for migrant workers, such as maternal care and child care, and improvement of recreational and educational opportunities. A regional office was established to direct the work.

The immediate goals of the committee were to improve housing, nutrition, and infant and maternal health, and to reduce delinquency. The long-term goals were to make the Hispanic people better Catholics, to improve educational and economic opportunities, and to eliminate discrimination and prejudice. These problems existed not only in society at large but also within the Catholic Church. In California, Anglo Catholics withdrew their children from parochial schools when they were opened to Mexican children.[15]

The bishops decided to begin special programs to defend against Protestant proselytism, which they saw as widespread. Almost every report by the committee mentioned the progress made in that area. In 1946, for example, it mentioned that *Somos Catolicos* (we are Catholics) posters had been printed and distributed to Spanish-speaking people. "Pastors will urge members of their flock to display these stickers on their front doors as means of discouraging Jehovah's Witnesses and other house-to-house proselytizers."[16]

But more important, the bishops formed their committee and established the councils and the regional office because *they* had changed. While in a previous time they had claimed that their proper sphere was the spiritual realm—to prepare the faithful for life after death—now they felt impelled to take a stronger role in seeking social justice. Perhaps it was because they had realized their inconsistency in this regard. In the case of the Irish, for example, the church had fought hard to over-come prejudice and to help the workers organize into labor unions. The bishops and clergy did not beg off, as they did when facing the injustice suffered by Hispanics, by claiming that the business of the church was not of this world.

Now the bishops asked that better wages be paid to Mexi-can American farm workers; that pit privies be eliminated in the barrios; that water, lights, and sewers be installed; and that streets be paved. The committee helped pastors to open employment bureaus, conduct naturalization classes, and organize Catholic War Veterans. The leaders among the bishops were Archbishop Lucey, an early advocate for Mexican American rights, and Samuel Cardinal Stritch of Chicago, who was head of the American Board of Catholic Missions, the chief source of funds for the committee's programs. During a visit to Texas, he had been "horrified at the kind of life most Mexicans lived. Their condition seemed to him worse than that of Negroes of the old South." His offer to seek funds "to attack these funda-mental ignominies" made the programs of the Bishops' Committee for the Spanish Speaking possible.[17]

Growth of the Church of the Poor

The key event in the growth and spread of the Hispanic population in the United States during the first part of the twenti-eth century was the Mexican Revolution, which began in 1910. It was the bloodiest war in the Western Hemisphere, lasting ten years and causing far more casualties than the American Civil War. It took more than a million lives and caused hundreds of thousands of refugees to leave the country. Moreover, it was followed by another ten years of turmoil, including religious persecution and the Cristero War between lay Catholics and the government from 1926 to 1929. Between 1910 and 1925 the United States admitted 660,000 Mexicans legally, while an estimated 300,000 came without permission.

In addition to immigrants who came to stay, in the 1880s Mexicans began coming for temporary work when the railroads, the mining companies, and agricultural enterprises began recruiting workers to replace the Chinese excluded by the Chinese Exclusion Act of 1882. World War I increased the need for such workers. As a result, the Bureau of Immigration changed its rules in 1918 to admit Mexicans for work in agriculture, the railroads, the mines, and construction. A total of 72,862 workers entered between 1917 and 1921. During World War II the State Department negotiated an agreement with the government of Mexico to permit the entry of Mexican *braceros*, as such workers came to be called, for seasonal work in agriculture. Between 1942, when the arrangement was made, and 1964, when it was finally canceled by Congress, 5.2 million Mexican workers participated in the program. According to the US Department of Labor's Bureau of Employment Security, during the peak year, 1956, a total of 445,197 *braceros* worked on farms from coast to coast. These legal programs, in turn, stimulated illegal migration, for there were many more applicants in Mexico than were accepted. Entry was easy until 1924 because the border with Mexico was open. At that time Congress established the Border Patrol, with a $1 million appropriation authorizing the hiring of 450 employees.[18] Enforcement was stepped up after World War II, and entry became more difficult.

When jobs became scarce or the economy declined, the authorities deported large numbers of Mexicans. In the first big expulsion, between 1920 and 1921, vigilantes encouraged by labor leaders and politicians terrorized Mexicans, causing the repatriation of 100,000. During the Great Depression of the 1930s, hundreds of thousands were sent to Mexico in order to save on welfare costs. As a result, the Mexican population in the United States declined from 630,000 to 377,000 in 1940.[19] The deportations originated in many cities on the West Coast and in the Midwest. In Detroit the Mexican consulate arranged for the departure of the Mexicans. Between 1931 and 1934 the Los Angeles Department of Social Service hired fifteen special trains, each transporting about one thousand people to Mexico City. Many of those deported were citizens or legal immigrants. The church remained silent in the face of such injustice. *The Tidings*, the diocesan newspaper of the Archdiocese of Los Angeles, carried only one small item on the repatriations.

During the first three decades of the twentieth century Hispanics experienced more violence than ever before. It seemed as though "open season" had been declared along the border.[20] From 1908 to 1925 as many as five thousand civilians—the exact number will never be known—died in lawlessness so widespread that a federal official warned the governor of Texas that action would have to be taken to protect the victims.

Often those responsible for the violence were the Texas Rangers, who had evolved from "ranging companies" organized in 1823 to repel Indian attacks. Though the Texas Rangers have been idolized as heroes of the West, an investigation in 1919 revealed that they had committed murder, intimidation, torture, flogging, and displayed a widespread disregard for the law.[21] One historian said the Texas Rangers "waged persecution," including threatened castration and legalized murder. Though he said some of the violence may have been understandable because they dealt with some of the cruelest outlaws who ever lived, "enough of this reprisal fell on people innocent of any crime but that of being Mexican."[22]

Time magazine reported that during World War II "the Rangers became little more than terrorists, a racist army for the purpose of intimidating Mexicans on both sides of the border."[23] The rangers often made raids into Mexico to bring back cattle and horses allegedly stolen from Texas ranchers. One time a troop looking for rustlers executed all the men of a Mexican village in the mistaken belief that they were the thieves. On other occasions they drove Mexican Americans away to make more land available for Anglo Americans. The rangers had the "visceral belief that the Anglo had exclusive rights to the political, educational and economic processes."[24] There is no record that the bishops of the Southwest protested against the epidemic of violence during that period.

Mexican Migration to the Midwest and East

Until the beginning of the twentieth century the Mexican American population of the United States had largely remained in the states acquired by conquest more than fifty years earlier—Texas, New Mexico, Arizona, California, and the fringes of states bordering them. But soon after the turn of the century, colonies began to spring up in many parts of the Midwest and even in the East. The Hispanic population of Kansas went from 71 Mexicans in 1900 to 8,429 in 1910 and 13,770 in 1920; Michigan increased from fewer than 100 in 1900 to more than 8,000 by the end of World War I; Illinois went from 156 in 1900 to 4,032 in 1920; and Nebraska went from 27 in 1900 to 3,611 in 1920. Even New York registered an increase from 353 in 1900 to 2,999 in 1920. There were few states that did not receive immigrants from Mexico between the beginning of the century and 1930. Between 1926 and 1927 money orders were sent to Mexico from forty-four of the forty-eight states.

Mexicans now used the Santa Fe Trail, the route used by traders and trappers to infiltrate New Mexico during the Mexican period, going the other way. Many of them came to work on the railroads. As early as 1907 they began to work as track laborers in Illinois. By 1910, 21 percent of the maintenance forces of the Santa Fe, Rock Island, and Galesburg and Aurora divisions of the Burlington Railroad were Mexican. Those percentages increased to 75 percent of the Santa Fe workers in 1927 and 80 percent of Burlington's by 1928. Others worked in meat-packing houses, steel mills, tanneries, and cement plants. In 1928 Mexicans were 12 percent of the workers in eight large plants of basic industries.

Heretofore, the migrants or immigrants who had come north to the United States had settled in the Southwest and worked in agriculture. As they traveled to the Midwest and other areas as agricultural workers, some of them gradually left farm work to settle in small towns. But the Mexican immigrants who came during the first three decades of the twentieth century were recruited directly into industrial jobs in the big cities, according to agreements with the Mexican government. For example, in 1923 the Bethlehem Steel Company brought at its own expense 912 men, 29 women, and 7 children from Mexico's central plateau to work at its plants in Bethlehem, Pennsylvania, Lackawanna, Ohio, and other places. The company's agreement with the consul general guaranteed wages and other benefits, including quarters and transportation back home for those who worked at least a year.[25] Similarly, the president of a steel company in Chicago brought several groups of Mexican workers from Chihuahua because he owned land there and knew the people.[26]

The recruitment of Mexicans became necessary after Congress passed the quota law, limiting the number of people from any nationality who could immigrate to the United States to 3 percent of those already in the country by 1910. The limitations, which did not apply to Canada, Cuba, Haiti, the Dominican Republic, Mexico, and Central and South America, sharply curtailed entries from Eastern Europe. That opened up many jobs in industry and agriculture to Mexicans and Mexican Americans.

Catholics and their pastors did not usually welcome the Mexicans in the Midwest and East. Priests said the Mexicans were superstitious and attached too much significance to small devotions. "We have shut out the European immigrant and have accepted the uncivilized Mexican in his place," a priest in Gary, Indiana, said. He charged that there were 560 communists in

Gary and most of them were Mexicans and Russians. He also complained that the Mexicans could not be Americanized.[27] Despite the tensions, the church provided aid to the Mexicans in time of need.

At the same time Mexicans were arriving in the Midwest from Mexico, Puerto Ricans were beginning to move to large eastern cities and, in smaller numbers, to work in agriculture in the East. The first migration occurred in 1900 when many went to Hawaii to work on the pineapple plantations. Between 1900 and 1909, however, only two thousand came to the mainland. They did not start to come in large numbers until 1917, when Congress made Puerto Ricans United States citizens, in time for many of them to serve in the Armed Forces during World War I. After the war few of the veterans returned to the Island; the majority settled in New York, where a small community already existed. The migration increased slowly through the first four decades of the twentieth century. Between 1920 and 1929, forty-two thousand came; between 1930 and 1940, eighteen thousand. The true exodus would not be until the period following World War II; New York, where more than one million would eventually settle, had only seventy thousand Puerto Ricans in 1940.

The Archdiocese of New York reacted to the growing number of Puerto Ricans (and other Hispanics, including Mexicans) by opening national chapels: Our Lady of Guadalupe in 1902, Our Lady of Esperanza in 1912, La Milagrosa in 1926, and Holy Agony in 1930. Our Lady of Pilar, founded in 1859, served the Hispanics who lived in Brooklyn. These chapels were "halfway stations" to provide the sacraments to the Spanish-speaking people until they could learn enough English to assimilate into territorial parishes. Many Puerto Ricans had the feeling that because they spoke a foreign language, they were considered to be not fully Catholic.[28]

The new Hispanic residents of the Midwest and East were welcomed neither in society nor in the churches. They encountered discrimination in restaurants, bars, and barbershops, and in employment. Farm workers, however, received the worst treatment. They were welcome only as long as there were crops to be planted, cultivated, or harvested. What happened in one Michigan county was typical of many areas. When the harvest was over, the sheriff rounded up any stragglers and told them to leave. "There is tacit agreement among all groups in the community that the migrants must be out of the area by October," said one report.[29]

In this period the Hispanic population was gradually migrating to the cities. Until the 1930s the Hispanics in the Southwest were largely a rural people. After World War II, however, they were one of the most urbanized groups in the United States. Several factors influenced the transformation. One was drought, another the Great Depression, and most decisive, World War II.

The war gave many the opportunity to acquire new skills and improve their earning capacity. Their performance exposed the oft-repeated lie that Hispanics were incapable of anything but common labor. The next generation would have a better chance to receive a good education. But these gains were not without cost. A people previously used to monocultural isolation found itself in an environment of cultural conflict and often violence.

In 1931 a presidential commission on law enforcement said that the police in East Chicago, where Mexican colonies were established in the first decade of the century, put Mexicans "into the calaboose" even if they had only a breath of liquor or laughed too loud at a party. "The police are bad to Mexicans," the report stated. "They do not wait for an explanation but catch every Mexican they suspect and hit him over the head."[30] Gratuitous violence, often from the police but sometimes from citizens, was a common hazard of urban life for Hispanics.

Sometimes there was mass violence, as in Los Angeles during World War II. In August 1942, police ostensibly combating youth gangs blockaded streets, stopped every car and every pedestrian, and arrested 600 youths, of whom 175 were charged with suspicion of crimes ranging from assault to robbery to auto theft. Any object that could be used in an assault—for instance, tire irons or tools in the trunks of cars—was viewed as evidence of criminality.

The campaign against Mexicans, abetted by inflammatory news stories, finally resulted in a riot in June 1943. Thousands of soldiers, sailors, and Marines, supposedly retaliating for the beating of eleven sailors by a Mexican American gang, rampaged through the streets of Los Angeles for an entire week. They assaulted hundreds of Mexican American youths and some adults while police watched, only to move in later to club and arrest the victims. When there was no one to attack, the servicemen sacked businesses. The disturbances were called the Zoot Suit Riots for the pleated, high-waisted pants and long coats worn by gang members who were the supposed targets. But the victims included children as young as twelve and even mothers trying to protect them.

In the investigations that followed, public officials tried to absolve themselves for doing nothing to prevent or stop the violence. The press tried to justify its prejudicial reporting. The investigators, however, found that the police set off the violence to help the cause of an officer named Dixon, who was coming to trial for kicking a drunk to death in the central jail. "By staging a fake demonstration of the alleged necessity for harsh police methods, it was hoped the jury would acquit Dixon," a journalist-historian wrote.[31] In other cities across the country there were less newsworthy incidents attributable to the same cause: the resistance of Anglo Americans to the Hispanic urban settlers.

The Struggle to Organize

The opening of the twentieth century marked the beginning of the struggle of Hispanics to win their rights in society. Anglo Americans would soon see behavior that would challenge the myth of the Mexican Americans as a docile people, even though half a century of violence and oppression had indeed made them a people who would endure in silence. It was a mechanism for survival. As novelist Mary Gordon wrote in relation to the Irish, "Silence too is another form of protective coloration not unknown by the oppressed."[32] But the new behavior, militant and demanding, indicated that the Hispanics were changing, gaining courage and confidence. Injustice rankles, and sooner or later an oppressed people is bound to rise. But another cause was the arrival of immigrants who had not been conquered. It was perhaps they who made the greater efforts to organize Hispanics, especially in the fields, orchards, and vineyards. For eight years the Industrial Workers of America, founded in 1905 and dubbed the Wobblies, tried to organize farm workers in California. But their leaders were thrown in jail, sometimes unjustly convicted, and their efforts ended in failure. Mass arrests and deportations led to the same fate for the first Mexican union, the Confederación de Uniones Campesinos in 1927, which had three thousand members in twenty locals in California. The Cannery and Agricultural Workers Union, which went on strike in the 1930s, fell victim to vigilante groups, the police, and the courts. In Vacaville forty masked men took six strike leaders out of jail, flogged them, and then clipped their heads with sheep shears and poured red enamel over them. In Pixley bullets riddled a union building, killing a husband and wife. No one was punished for those crimes, even though some of the perpetrators were positively identified. Instead, eight union leaders served two years in prison.

The response to a strike by cantaloupe harvesters who walked off their jobs in California's Imperial Valley in 1928 was typical of many other encounters. The sheriff falsely accused the strikers of being communists and arrested four leaders for disturbing the peace. Then he closed the offices of the union, declared future strikes unlawful, told the Mexicans they should go back to Mexico if they were not satisfied in the United

States, arrested a newspaper vender critical of his tactics, and even prohibited Mexicans from gathering for any reason. The courts set high bail for the strikers.

But it was not only those charged with law enforcement who opposed the organization of the farm workers. When Congress passed the National Labor Relations Act in 1935, it excluded farm workers from its benefits. Government agencies such as the Immigration and Naturalization Service sometimes relaxed controls at the border to let in undocumented workers to defeat strikes. No one really believed that the workers were communists; that was just a convenient pretext for putting them down. What was at issue was the one-sided social contract with the Mexicans and Mexican Americans. They had a place in society only as long as they accepted their marginal status. Society condoned the shoddy treatment of farm workers with assertions that they were happy following the crops, that they were getting much better wages than they would have earned in Mexico—even if they were American citizens and had never lived there—and that they were being treated justly.

The struggle in the mines was as difficult as in the fields. Troops were called out when Hispanic copper miners tried to organize in Arizona in 1903. They were protesting the fact that Anglo Americans were paid more for the same kind of work. The mining company sealed up the mine and told the strikers to go home to Mexico. In 1917, when copper miners went on strike again, vigilantes hired by their employer forced 1,186 miners to board railroad boxcars and shipped them to Columbus, New Mexico. When several thousand coal miners employed by the Gallup-American Company in New Mexico went on strike in the mid-1930s, the area was placed under martial law, even though there had been no violence. There followed a mass eviction of workers, a bloody riot, and mass arrests. Jesús Pallares, a miner from Chihuahua, then organized the Liga Obrera de Habla Española. With eight thousand members, it forced the authorities to abandon criminal charges. But Pallares was deported. Labor troubles due to unequal pay continued into the 1940s. The mines were sometimes closed so that new workers could be hired at lower wages when they reopened.

In San Antonio thousands of pecan shellers went on strike in 1938. The issue was wages, only $2 a week in 1934 and only slightly better afterward than on the piecework system. When the workers struck, police beat and jailed them. The police chief closed their soup kitchen. His tactics were so repressive that the governor of Texas criticized his conduct. Yet the archbishop of San Antonio, Arthur J. Drossaerts, refused to support the strike. Instead, he commended the police for acting against "Communist influences."[33]

Besides labor unions, many other civic mutual aid organizations came into being in the twentieth century. Mutual aid societies flourished by the dozens wherever Hispanics lived. In serving a variety of needs, such as insurance, burial services, aid in emergencies, and the like, they provided cultural continuity and ethnic identity for the Mexican Americans.[34] Some of the mutual aid societies also worked for civil rights. One of the most widely known civil rights organizations was the Primero Congreso Mexicanista, organized in 1911 to fight discrimination and repression, particularly segregation in schools. Another was the Congreso de Pueblos de Habla Española, established in 1939. The most interesting note about this group, which fought against race and class discrimination, is that it had not only Mexican American representation from the Southwest but Puerto Rican representation from the New York area. A third civil rights organization, La Liga Protectora, was formed in 1914 in Phoenix, Arizona, to oppose state legislation that would have placed limits on the hiring of Mexican Americans. The most important civic organization that appeared during the first half of the twentieth century was the League of United Latin American Citizens, established in 1929. Its overall goal was to make Hispanics good American citizens by encouraging them to learn English and adopt the values of the United States. It soon found itself in the midst of the struggle for civil rights. Its legal efforts led to the desegregation of public schools in Texas and California. It also attacked the exclusion of Mexican Americans from juries and founded schools for preschool children that became the model for the Headstart program.

Some historians see this period as a second defeat (the first being after 1846) for the Spanish-speaking peoples.[35] Those writers see the Hispanics once again withdrawing into cultural isolation. But, in reality, the Hispanics by the end of World War II had spread all over the nation. The old barrios of the Southwest could no longer hold them. They had broadened their horizons so much that they could no longer be happy in isolation. They had gained skills, but more important, a new estimate of their possibilities. They would never go back.

Part IV

The Church of the Poor Comes of Age

Chapter 5

The Struggle for Rights

Except as people sitting passively in the pews, Hispanics had virtually no institutional representation in the church in the late 1940s. There were few Hispanic priests because up to then little or no recruiting of Hispanic vocations had taken place. Spaniards were the largest group of Spanish-speaking priests, but their culture and that of the Hispanic people of the Southwest were not the same. The Spaniards were apt to judge the people they served as backward. After three centuries of virtual isolation, there was a cultural gap if not a chasm. Few priests had come from Latin America with the immigrants. After the revolution Mexico was left with only 230 priests; it could ill afford to part with any of them. A similar situation prevailed in Puerto Rico, where the big migration to the mainland was already under way.

The Hispanic clergyman, native or immigrant, was not in significant roles. The office of the Bishops' Committee for Hispanics was headed by Anglo priests until 1967, when Father Henry Casso of San Antonio was named executive secretary.[1] At that time, too, a highly regarded Mexican American priest, Patricio Flores, was the state chairman of the committee. Hispanics were absent from the chanceries and from the offices of the National Catholic Welfare Conference, the predecessor of the current United States Catholic Conference. There was one exception, however, and that was Father John García. Beginning in 1949 he was one of four priests who spent twelve years going up and down the valleys of California ministering to the farm workers, until then sadly neglected by parishes and dioceses.

Similarly, Hispanic laity was absent from leadership posts in chanceries, hospitals, schools, universities—or any other institution. Even in parish life Hispanics seldom held the top posts of organizations, if they were included at all. The only thing they directed in the parish in Brighton, Colorado (where the author grew up), was their own bazaar, which was separate from a similar festival held by the Anglo American parishioners.

The number of native Hispanic clergy grew slowly during the 1950s and 1960s. One reason was that few Hispanics qualified for admission to the seminaries. Few Mexican Americans, for instance, graduated from high school. Those who did often went to inferior schools, with the result that the rare ones who applied to the seminary often could not pass the entrance tests. Or if they did, they soon found themselves in academic difficulties. What's more, seminaries were not friendly places for the Hispanics. David Gómez, a former Paulist priest, said he became withdrawn in the seminary because he was ignored by his Anglo classmates. Living on the periphery of the white world but not invited in, he concluded that the promise of acceptance and equality was "a total lie and a double-cross."[2] Father Paul Baca, a priest from Albuquerque, recounted a comment by Denver's Archbishop Urban J. Vehr, who had come to give a talk at St. Thomas Seminary, a regional institution run by the Vincentians in Denver. In the presence of two Hispanic deacons Archbishop Vehr said, "The reason I don't have Mexican seminarians is that they just don't meet my standards."[3] Behind such views was the belief that Hispanics were of such weak faith that they could not be priests. Another reason, seldom articulated, was that the bishops also subscribed to the idea that Hispanics were an inferior people. They felt that the priesthood, like the officer class in the Armed Forces, was for whites only.

The Civil Rights Movement

The postwar period in the United States was marked by increasing integration. In civil society the Supreme Court ruled in 1954 in its landmark case *Brown vs. Board of Education* that segregated schools were unconstitutional. The battle has been portrayed as one of blacks versus whites, but it also affected Hispanics. In less publicized cases the League of United Latin American Citizens had won important state victories that had set the stage for *Brown vs. Board of Education*. In 1945, in *Mendez vs. Orange County* (California), a federal court in San Francisco banned segregation of children of Mexican or Latin descent "for reasons of race, color or national origin." Then, in 1948, a court in Texas ruled for the first time that it was unlawful and unconstitutional to segregate Mexican children in the public schools of Texas.[4] Integration began to take place not only in the schools but also in other public accommodations.

The Catholic Church followed the same trends, trying to bring its various ethnic groups together, but the process actually had begun much earlier. The church had begun phasing out its national parishes in the 1920s. This move was influenced by nativist prejudice that had led to the enactment of laws limiting immigration to a percentage of those groups already in the United States. In 1916 there were 4,765 foreign-language parishes, 47 percent of the total; by 1948 the number had decreased to 1,535.[5]

The leaders of the Catholic Church and their followers felt that they had to be "100 percent American." That conviction led Cardinal George Mundelein of Chicago to order in 1916 that foreign-language textbooks be dropped from the Catholic schools. Such Americanization efforts were also directed at Hispanics. In 1918 the National Catholic War Council gave $50,000 to Bishop Cantwell of Los Angeles for Americanization work, which *The Tidings*, the diocesan newspaper, declared "preeminently a Catholic responsibility."[6]

Americanization, however, proved to be a tragic mistake. Hispanic leadership, in the church or in society, has come from two groups least affected by American culture, immigrants and long-time residents from areas such as New Mexico, south Texas, and parts of California where Hispanic culture was not overwhelmed.

The 1960s also brought civil rights legislation that had an impact on the church, specifically the Civil Rights Act and the Voting Rights Act, both enacted in 1964. These laws were a response to the highly publicized struggle for civil rights by blacks and, though less well known, also by Hispanics. Another national program that would force the church to pay more attention to its Hispanic members was the War on Poverty declared by President Lyndon Johnson in 1964.

In the church great changes were taking place as well. The bishops at Vatican II declared that the church had to take a stronger role in the world. God had spoken in the history of all peoples; thus God's word ought to be discovered and respected in different cultures. Suddenly, Americanization, previously an important element in the church's ministry to Hispanics, no longer seemed wise. Among other reforms Vatican II decreed that the liturgy should be celebrated in the vernacular instead of Latin. As far as Hispanics were concerned, that meant that Mass should be offered in Spanish and that their religious traditions should be respected rather than discarded in favor of the religion of the "melting pot."

At the same time the council documents demanding a stronger institutional commitment to social justice showed how far the church had to move to fulfill its responsibility. This insight was enhanced by the documents of Medellín, the historic meeting of Latin American bishops in 1968 that elaborated on the message of Vatican II. In particular, the commitment of the church to a special "option for the poor" contrasted starkly with the identification of the US bishops with the economic interests of the middle and upper classes and the views of the political elite.

Struggle within the Church

By the mid-1960s there was a growing conflict between the *Movimiento*, as the Mexican American civil rights movement was known, and the church. In general, Hispanics objected to efforts to deprive them of their language and culture. Some resorted to symbolic acts demonstrating that they and their religion were not being respected. In Mission, Texas, on the Sunday after Christmas in 1969, about one hundred Mexican Americans painted the statue of the Blessed Virgin brown.[7] In 1974 members of the militant Brown Berets took over the parish church in Brighton, Colorado, and refused to let anyone enter until the pastor agreed to offer a Mass in Spanish each weekend.

Hispanic clergy and religious women and brothers also became aware that their training, whether by design or not, had caused them to reject their culture. Furthermore, they found themselves in situations where they could not serve their own people and where, in some cases, they were not permitted to do so. Father Patricio Flores, who was to become the first Mexican American bishop, said, "When I was ordained, I was sent to a parish where I was asked not to use Spanish to communicate with people who did not understand English."[8] A survey of Spanish-speaking brothers showed that only 8 percent were in full-time ministry to their own people and 21 percent in part-time work. Only 25 of 961 Hispanic sisters were in ministry to Hispanics.

Hispanic priests, sisters, and brothers who asked to be assigned to Hispanic ministry encountered difficulties. John Cardinal Cody of Chicago rejected the request of Servite Father Alberto Gallegos and another priest who asked to be reassigned to Hispanic ministry. That reaction was common. Father Juan Romero of Los Angeles recalled, "In my first parish in Los Angeles I was not permitted to celebrate Mass or preach in Spanish in spite of the fact that 80 percent of the confessions

I heard each week in the parish were in Spanish."[9] To many pastors, Romero indicated, it was more important to teach English than to proclaim the gospel in a meaningful way. There was great anger among Hispanics when they realized that they had been unwitting accomplices in the neglect of their people by the institutional church. As a consequence, some gave up their vocations and returned to the laity. Others opted to confront and demand that the church fulfill its responsibility to Hispanics.

In time, many of the Hispanic clergy and religious men and women were able to gain assignments that permitted them to minister to their own people. That goal, however, could not be accomplished without organization. It also required a transformation of their own lives. Originally assigned to English-speaking parishes with the explanation that they had been ordained or professed to serve everyone, these Hispanic men and women gradually lost their culture and, when they finally succeeded in being reassigned to Hispanic ministry, they were often no longer able to relate to their own people.

The Hispanics in the United States have been subjected to a process that communicated in countless ways the message that they and their culture were inferior. This has led, in extreme cases, to self-hatred; more often, it has resulted in contempt for their own culture and people. The "successful" Hispanic tried to escape to the Anglo world, hoping to be accepted. Hispanics who entered the seminary or religious novitiate often wanted nothing to do with their own people when they were ordained or professed. What the *Movimiento* did for Hispanics was to reverse that process, to make them acknowledge their background and, better, to be proud of it.

"We are not ashamed of what we are," said Father Virgil Elizondo, a diocesan priest from Texas who became the leading Mexican American theologian. "We are proud of the heritage we have received from our parents and ancestors. We are proud to be descendants of our great Indian and European forefathers.[10]

Not all Hispanic clergy made the conversion, but those who became the leaders of the Hispanic church did. They became the true representatives of their people.

PADRES: Champions of Justice

One of the organizations that came into being was PADRES (Priests Associated for Religious, Educational, and Social Rights). On October 7–9, 1969, fifty Mexican American priests from seven states and the District of Columbia met in San Antonio. At the conclusion of their meeting they called a press conference to announce that they had formed a new national organization to transmit "'the cry of our people to the decision-makers of the Catholic Church in America."[11] The membership approved twenty-seven resolutions to present to the National Conference of Catholic Bishops at its annual meeting in Washington the following month. Father Ralph Ruiz was elected national chairman, and Father Edmundo Rodríguez, SJ, was named national vice-regent.

PADRES made clear that it would be the voice of the voiceless Hispanics. In a letter of October 15, 1969, to Archbishop Francis J. Furey of San Antonio, Father Ruiz wrote, "We feel that we have a unique role as spokesmen within the Church for Mexican American and Spanish-speaking Catholics in the United States because most of us share the same language, culture, social mores and religious values of our people."

Among the resolutions were the following:

- that native Hispanic bishops be named in areas with heavy concentrations of Spanish-speaking people;
- that native Spanish-speaking priests be appointed immediately as pastors in large Spanish-speaking communities;
- that consideration be given to subsidizing low-income parishes from a national Catholic source;

- that high priority be given to inner-city projects involving priests more deeply in the day-to-day economic, social, and religious life of the people;
- that the church use its influence on behalf of the striking California grape pickers; and
- that seminary recruitment and education be expanded to include programs adapted to the needs of Mexican American seminarians and parishioners.

PADRES was especially harsh on the subject of vocations. Another letter to Archbishop Furey, dated October 9, 1969, said: "We *emphatically* reject as myth that the Mexican American has not given himself in sufficient numbers to the priestly ministry in the Church. All of us experienced during our seminary days the anxieties of many of our contemporaries who were forced out of the seminary one way or the other." The letter went on to say that there had been systematic rejection, concluding, "We do not want to judge the motives of those who forced them out or kept them out, but we do know the fact that they were forced out or kept out."[12]

The Struggle of Las Hermanas

About a year later Hispanic religious women began the process of organizing too. One of the catalysts was Victory Noll Sister Gregoria Ortega, who singlehandedly tried to improve the lives of Hispanics in the Diocese of Abilene. Alone, with no title or support from the clergy, she faced down policemen, judges, school principals, and school boards to fight for better education and working conditions. Some priests attacked her from the pulpit, and eventually the bishop asked her to leave the diocese.

Sister Gloria Gallardo, who worked as a community organizer and catechist in San Antonio's inner-city barrios, joined Ortega. After years of working beside people struggling to maintain hope amid chronic unemployment, health problems, and malnutrition, Gallardo decided not only to dedicate herself exclusively to her own people, but also to help other religious women to make the same commitment. She said there were "innumerable cases" of sisters who had asked their superiors to be allowed to work among their own people and had been denied permission.[13]

On April 2–4, 1971, fifty nuns from eight states gathered in Houston for the first meeting of Las Hermanas. Representing twenty religious congregations, the sisters decided that the sole purpose of their new organization would be "more effective and active service of the Hispanic people by using the expertise, knowledge, and experience of religious women in the fields of education, health, pastoral work, and sociology."[14] The assembly declared:

> Sisters throughout the country have seen a tremendous gap between the relevancy of our consecration and our service to the People of God, especially the poor. We have searched for ways of closing this gap and have felt the urgency to become more attuned to the needs of the community so as to render better service to our apostolate. We, as Spanish-speaking Sisters, are greatly concerned with the plight of La Raza especially and are determined to better our efforts to meet their needs.[15]

One of the projects of Las Hermanas was to speak for hundreds of Mexican nuns who worked in seminaries, retreat houses, or colleges doing housekeeping, cooking, or other menial work. In one institution visited by Las Hermanas, each sister was receiving only fifty dollars a month. Such meager pay was going to Mexico to support impoverished congregations needing every cent to survive. Las Hermanas found that about half of these Mexican nuns would rather have been in catechetical work with Spanish-speaking people. Mexican nuns who came specifically to do such work often received little or no pay and were not even registered in the religious census because they were not citizens. "How can we as religious, priests, and bishops accuse the laymen of being unjust and exploiting our Mexican brothers when we are doing the same in the name of apostolic work?" asked Sister Carmelita Espinoza and Sister María de Jesús Ibarra of the Las Hermanas coordinating team. "Is it necessary to profess vows to be a waitress or a house maid?"[16] Las Hermanas began a program of educating Mexican nuns for the possibility of apostolic service, but the congregations in Mexico were nervous about losing the support, little as it was, from their members in domestic service in the United States.

The Mexican American Cultural Center

One of the effects of the organization of Hispanic clergy and religious was the founding of unique institutions to serve the Spanish-speaking people. One of the first was the Mexican American Cultural Center (MACC). It began in 1971 as a language institute because the promotion of the study of the Spanish language was the most critical need at the time. Six other institutes were added later. They dealt with culture, pastoral service, preparation of missionaries for Latin America, research and publications, leadership development, and media. Thousands of students came from all parts of the United States, Puerto Rico, and Central and South America. Many of the faculty members were PADRES and Las Hermanas members who worked for a minimal salary so that the institution would succeed.

The creative spirit behind MACC was its president, Father Virgil Elizondo. In 1970, while teaching at the Incarnate Word Pastoral Institute in San Antonio, Elizondo became convinced that the Hispanic people of the United States needed an institute of their own. The idea won enthusiastic approval from PADRES when it was presented at its annual retreat in Santa

Fe in February 1971. In September of the same year the Texas Catholic Conference gave its unanimous approval to a motion by vocation directors asking for the creation of the institution. With Archbishop Furey heading the steering committee, the archdiocese provided buildings and housing on the campus of Assumption Seminary for an annual rent of one dollar. Patricio Flores, who had become the first Hispanic bishop the previous year, was elected chairman of the board of directors. With his talent as a fundraiser, MACC was assured of survival. Eventually, MACC became the model for other pastoral centers for Hispanics. By 1988 such centers were in operation in Miami, New York, and South Bend, Indiana. At the beginning of the twenty-first century some had faded, but MACC and the Southeast Pastoral Institute in Miami still had strong, innovative programs.

This period also saw the development of other church-sponsored institutions concerned with Hispanic affairs. In the late 1960s Father John McCarthy, director of the national office for Hispanics, which developed out of the Southwest Office for the Spanish Speaking in the 1950s, convinced Archbishop Robert Lucey, the most influential member of the Bishops' Committee for the Spanish Speaking, that there should be a regional office in the Midwest. For some years Chicago had had a branch office of sorts, the Cardinal's Committee for the Spanish Speaking, organized in 1955. But an organization with broader scope was needed. The new office was established in Lansing, Michigan, in 1967. It served dioceses in Ohio, Indiana, Michigan, Wisconsin, Illinois, Iowa, and North Dakota. The person hired to head the new office was a Hispanic layman, Rubén Alfaro, a former migrant worker and barber, who traveled throughout the region encouraging dioceses to establish departments for Hispanics. He insisted that members of the laity, preferably Spanish speaking, should head these offices. His suggestions were usually followed, with the result that many lay Hispanics became involved in the apostolate.

Hispanic offices were being organized in many other dioceses. As in the Midwest, many of them were headed by Hispanic lay people. It was the only place on chancery staffs, almost always composed of Anglo Americans, that Hispanics had a place. These offices, however, were a mixed blessing. While they promised that at least token efforts would be made to serve Hispanics, the result was that other chancery offices tended to do nothing, assuming that ministry to Hispanics was not their responsibility.

In 1967 the bishops of California established the West Coast Regional Office for Hispanics. Unlike the Midwest office, which has continued in some form since its founding, the West Coast office lasted only a few years. The main problem was that the two archdioceses, Los Angeles and San Francisco, refused to go along with the program. Regional offices were eventually established (or reestablished) in all parts of the country. The office established by the bishops' committee in 1945 was given national scope in 1964 but did not come under Hispanic leadership until 1967. At that time Antonio Tinajero, a layman, was hired as director. In 1971 he was replaced by Pablo Sedillo, a New Mexican with a liking for politics. At that time the office was moved to Washington and made a division of the USCC's Department of Social Development and World Peace. Sedillo's job was to lobby in behalf of Hispanics among the different departments of the USCC, but before long he was also lobbying on Capitol Hill. His efforts among the bishops won budget approval to hire four professional assistants. One traveled the country giving workshops on basic Christian communities, while the others assumed responsibility for communications, for programs in the Northeast, and for programs in behalf of migrants.

A lack of direct communication with other divisions and departments, however, hampered the division. Finally, in 1974, due to pressure from Sedillo and from PADRES, the bishops created the secretariat for Hispanic Affairs, directly responsible to the National Conference of Catholic Bishops. Sedillo headed the Secretariat until the 1990s, when he was succeeded by another Hispanic layman, Ronaldo Cruz, from Arizona.

The First Hispanic Bishop

By that time much more significant changes had taken place, thanks to the courage of Archbishop Francis J. Furey of San Antonio. He did what no other bishop before had dared to do: he requested that a Mexican American be ordained a bishop. Shortly after being named archbishop of San Antonio in 1969, Furey requested that Father Patricio Flores, a man he had never met, be named his auxiliary. When the authorities asked for two more names, he returned the paperwork with Flores's name written three times. He explained: "If I had three Mexican Americans who were equally qualified, I would write them all down. To get an auxiliary bishop in Texas, we don't want to go to California. The auxiliary should be a native."[17]

Nevertheless, Furey had to sell his choice to the apostolic delegate, Archbishop Luigi Raimundi. "I told him we should have a Mexican American here because of the fact that we have so many [Hispanics] here. But the delegate said he had to make a report to Rome, and they would ask who started this and does he know what he is doing. So, of course, I had to do a lot of pushing because, as you can imagine, a breakthrough in the Catholic Church is not easy." Reminded that there had never been a Mexican American bishop, Furey replied: "That is an argument for me, not against me."[18]

That is how it came to pass that on May 5, 1970, Patricio Flores was ordained a bishop. (The date was doubly significant for all Mexican Americans. Cinco de Mayo is the anniversary of the day in 1862 when a ragtag Mexican army defeated invading French forces in Puebla, restoring self-respect after the debacle of the Mexican War.) The ordination, held at the San Antonio convention center because no church was large enough, drew eight thousand people. Cesar Chavez, the leader of the farm workers in California, read one of the scripture passages for the Mass. Thus it was that almost a century after the first black bishop was ordained in the United States (James Augustine Healy, ordained a bishop in 1875), Mexican Americans had their first prelate.

Flores was a true representative of the poor. He was born in Ganado, Texas, the sixth of nine children of a migrant family. As a boy, he and his family followed the crops north. Sometimes they lived in sheds. Attending classes only part time because of the demands of migrant work, Flores dropped out of school by the tenth grade. He had felt the sting of discrimination, the gnawing of hunger, the despair of defeat. When he first expressed an interest in the priesthood, the priest in whom he confided turned him away. And when he finally won admission to the seminary, thanks to the intercession of a sister and the goodwill of the bishop, he had to shine the shoes of his classmates to earn the money he needed for incidentals.

Between 1970 and the fall of 1988 twenty Hispanic bishops were ordained, half of them immigrants. Two were from Mexico, two from Cuba, two from Spain, one from Ecuador, two from Puerto Rico, and one from Venezuela. The others were native-born Hispanics. None, immigrant or native, showed the commitment to the poor that Flores did. For his first few years, before he became the ordinary of El Paso and then the archbishop of San Antonio, he was in a sense bishop to all Mexican Americans. Once again he followed the migrant trail to the Midwest and Northwest visiting squalid labor camps and bringing hope to the workers. When Cesar Chavez was jailed for defying unconstitutional court injunctions, Flores went to visit him. Once a grower who did not want him around barred his way with a shotgun aimed at his belly. But Flores was not intimidated.

Through Flores's support a powerful barrio federation—Communities Organized for Public Service (COPS)—came into being in San Antonio. It became a model for other such groups in Houston, El Paso, and Los Angeles.

Flores also spoke out on behalf of Hispanics in urban areas who suffered police violence or who were unjustly accused of crimes. Once he raffled off his episcopal ring for twenty-two hundred dollars to defend a twenty-one-year-old man charged with a murder he did not commit.

Aware of how difficult it is for the poor to finance higher education, he established the National Hispanic Scholarship Fund in 1975. It has raised millions of dollars to help Hispanics get through college. Flores also was a strong advocate for the *indocumentados* (illegal immigrants). He served for a number of years as chairman of the Texas Advisory Committee to the US Commission on Civil Rights, and he established the first diocesan office in the Southwest to deal with the problems of immigrants. Sometimes he personally tried to collect on the worthless paychecks issued by employers to undocumented workers. While visiting farm workers in California a few months after he was named bishop, he arrived in Los Angeles at the height of the 1970 Vietnam War Moratorium march. Mexican Americans, protesting the high casualties and the disproportion of Mexican Americans among front-line troops, gathered in a park one Sunday afternoon in August to hear speeches. Police attacked the crowd after a minor disturbance; several persons were killed, and many were injured. Only Mexican American priests ministered to the dying and the wounded, and the only bishop who would meet with the leaders was Flores, an act that earned a stern reprimand from the cardinal archbishop of Los Angeles and the apostolic delegate. He had trespassed on another bishop's territory!

In addition to his commitment to social justice in civil society, Flores worked hard to improve the lot of Hispanics in the church. On trips to Mexico he would keep an eye open to potential vocations. Once, in Guadalajara, after he had become archbishop, he noticed a young man standing outside the cathedral as he approached to celebrate Mass. The young man was still there when Flores emerged. So the archbishop walked up to him and asked: "When are you going to be ordained?" The young man, named David, said that once he had hoped to become a priest, but he had given up the dream because he felt that he had not lived a good life. The archbishop replied that he saw no impediment and invited him to study in a seminary in the United States. Today David is a priest in San Antonio.

By 1987, with scholarship money from the fund he created, fifteen men from Mexico had been ordained for service in the United States. In addition, he had been able to save the vocations of Hispanics who had run into problems in the seminary. One of them was Father Jerry Barnes, in 1988 the rector of Assumption Seminary in San Antonio. He had been turned away by a religious order when he was only a year short of ordination. Barnes, later bishop of the California Diocese of San Bernardino, was never told why he had been rejected; he guessed it was because he insisted on working with his own people.

Just as Flores encouraged Hispanics to organize in civil society, he strongly supported PADRES and Las Hermanas and other groups in the church. He was the second national chairman of PADRES.

Other Hispanic Bishops

One other bishop—Gilbert Chavez, auxiliary in the Diocese of San Diego—comes from a similar background. His father was a farm worker who picked grapes and oranges and harvested potatoes and other vegetables in San Bernardino, California. When Gilbert was fourteen years old, his father was killed in an accident. To support himself, Gilbert worked as a busboy in restaurants, as a packer in grocery stores, and as a laborer in the fields. He had to help support his family as well as pay his own way through Catholic high school. Like Flores, he suffered deprivation and discrimination.

As a priest, one of Chavez's jobs for four years was that of chaplain at a state rehabilitation center for drug addicts. In a newspaper interview for his episcopal ordination on June 21, 1974, he said: "I have accepted the challenge to serve the poor, the Spanish speaking, the Indians, blacks, and other minorities."

Unfortunately, Chavez did not have the same support from his ordinary that Flores had from Furey. Then, too, his rhetoric was less polished, more abrasive. In a few years he had been effectively silenced, assigned to a border parish. He continued to work with Hispanics in the diocese but had no influence beyond the small circle of his diocesan activities. His short-lived efforts to be prophetic had foreclosed any opportunity he might have had to be an ordinary.

The same fate awaited Bishop Juan Arzube, an Ecuadorian ordained bishop in 1971 to serve as an auxiliary in the Archdiocese of Los Angeles. His being named had created disappointment among Mexican Americans, who wanted one of their own. Nevertheless, he set out to prove that he was a worthy shepherd. He championed the cause of a young lawyer who had been arrested in a protest against the archdiocese on Christmas Eve in 1969. The State Bar Association had withheld accreditation for the lawyer, Ricardo Cruz, because he had been convicted of a misdemeanor as a result of the demonstration. The bishop spoke before the bar examiners and persuaded them to admit Cruz. He also made a courageous speech to the Catholic Press Association that stirred criticism from his brother bishops. Until his retirement in the 1990s he remained an auxiliary in the Archdiocese of Los Angeles.

One of the young priests Flores recommended for bishop was Ricardo Ramírez, who became his auxiliary and later the first bishop of a new diocese—Las Cruces, New Mexico. A Basilian who served as a missionary in Mexico and later as executive vice-president of the Mexican American Cultural Center, Ramírez quickly won respect in the National Conference of Catholic Bishops and became one of the most influential Hispanic bishops. He chaired the sessions of the NCCB during the debate over the historic pastoral "The Hispanic Presence:

Challenge and Commitment." He also played a leading role in the writing and editing of the national pastoral plan for Hispanic ministry approved unanimously by the bishops in November 1987. Following in Flores's footsteps, he served as chairman of the Bishops' Committee for the church in Latin America from 1985 to 1988 and was chosen over Cardinal Bernard Law of Boston as an alternate for the 1987 Synod on the Laity in Rome.

Ramírez also comes from a background of poverty and would have to be classified as an activist. But because he has always tempered strong support for the poor, especially immigrants, with a measure of prudence, he has avoided making enemies. Like Archbishop Robert Sanchez of Santa Fe, who served until 1993, he is among the most articulate of the Hispanic bishops. In the late 1980s he was probably the bishop most active on a national level. Through his participation in CEHILA he is widely known in intellectual circles throughout Latin America. He has served as administrative secretary of the commission and wrote historical papers about the Hispanic church in the United States.

If Flores was the model for the activists among Hispanic bishops, Archbishop Sanchez set the example for those who were called pastoralists.[19] Whatever mark they have made has been more within the institutional church than in civil society. Sanchez and Flores had contrasting backgrounds. Sanchez represented the middle class, the son of an Hispanic lawyer and a mother of Spanish and Irish stock. He studied at the Gregorian University in Rome, where he was ordained in 1959. Later he studied canon law at the Catholic University of America in Washington, D.C.

At first it appeared Sanchez would be an activist in the mold of Flores. After his episcopal ordination, attended by thirteen thousand people, he took up a collection for the farm workers and asked pastors to urge support for the grape boycott then being waged by the United Farm Workers. Nevertheless, it soon became evident that he was less inclined to become involved in the affairs of the world than Flores. For the Third National Encuentro in 1985, he devoted his homily at the opening Mass to Our Lady of Guadalupe. Flores, in the other hand, gave a blunt talk on how far Hispanics had yet to travel to gain equity in the church and in society.

Sometimes, however, Sanchez had no choice but to move out of the sphere he preferred. On February 2–3, 1980, a bloody prison riot in the New Mexico State Penitentiary left thirty-three prisoners dead and ninety severely injured. Twelve of the twenty-five corrections officers on duty were taken hostage and subjected to such indignities that they were unable to return to duty. The prison facility was virtually destroyed.[20] The archbishop was summoned to Santa Fe to lend his assistance. At considerable risk he went into the prison to remove the Blessed Sacrament from the chapel. But he played no role in the negotiations that eventually brought an end to the violence, for which some of the press was critical.

It was in the institutional church that Sanchez made his mark. He reconciled the Penitentes, alienated since the time of Archbishop Jean Lamy. He revived many of the traditions of the Hispanic people in the isolated villages of the diocese. He reversed the trend toward closing mission churches in small communities. And he reformed the seminary to make it more responsive to Spanish and Indian cultures. On a national level he headed the Ad Hoc Bishops' Committee for Hispanic Affairs for nine years, giving strong support to Pablo Sedillo in the Secretariat for Hispanic Affairs. But his career ended in disgrace in the early 1990s when, accused in a sex scandal involving young women, he resigned his post, virtually disappearing, although he remained a priest, living out of public view in religious houses around the country.

Many of the Hispanic bishops, loathe like Sanchez to confront issues of social justice, were cautious. Along the border it was a non-Hispanic, Bishop John Fitzpatrick of Brownsville, who was the strongest advocate for refugees. Ironically, many Hispanics voiced disappointment when he was appointed in

1971. Activist Mexican American priests and nuns were particularly critical of the appointment. At great personal cost Fitzpatrick committed the resources of his poor diocese to defend the rights of refugees and immigrants. He supported Casa Oscar Romero, which at one time sheltered as many as five hundred refugees in defiance of federal policies he considered unjust. Furthermore, he adopted a simple lifestyle that provided a model for other bishops.

Cardinal Roger Mahony of Los Angeles, especially in his early years when he was the bishop of Stockton, also demonstrated an admirable commitment to the poor. A few others, among them Archbishop John R. Quinn of San Francisco and William S. Skylstad of Yakima, also distinguished themselves.

One bishop who was very pastoral and who responded admirably in time of crisis was Agustín Román, auxiliary in the Archdiocese of Miami and himself a Cuban refugee. When Cuban prisoners rioted and seized control of federal prisons in Oakdale and Atlanta in the late 1980s, they demanded that he mediate between them and federal officials, who wanted to deport them to Cuba. Román, despite frail health, went to the prisons and negotiated a peaceful settlement. He dedicated himself to the Cuban people until his retirement in 2003.

Some of the Hispanic bishops, however, were virtually invisible in the National Conference of Catholic Bishops. They made news only when they were ordained and were not heard from afterward. They seldom spoke out at the bishops' meetings. Two were political reactionaries, supporting right-wing positions in Central America. As a group, Hispanic bishops failed, because of their differences, to create an effective lobby within the body of bishops. One said in 1988 that they could not even get together for a meeting.

By then, Hispanics did not seem as eager about having Hispanic bishops as they had been in the early 1970s. One of the leaders of PADRES, the Chicano priests' organization that lobbied so strongly for Hispanic bishops, said: "They [the National Conference of Catholic Bishops] beat us at our own game."[21] In the view of activist priests and nuns, the first four Hispanic bishops strongly supported their objectives, but those who came later were meek and mild. After that, the activist priests simply asked that whoever was selected be committed to the Hispanics. The assumption of PADRES and Las Hermanas had been that a Hispanic, by virtue of his ethnicity, would naturally take up the struggles of the people. It turned out to be an overly optimistic estimate. For some, it was a question of temperament. For others, there were barriers of ethnicity, class, ecclesiology, or political philosophy. A bishop from Spain, for example, brought a culture that harmonized with that of a Puerto Rican only in superficial ways. One or two of the native-born Hispanic bishops had assimilated to North American culture to the point that they hardly spoke the language or understood the longings and aspirations of, say, Mexican Americans. Some were middle class, and their values did not accord with those of farm workers or of the urban poor.

As a group, Hispanic bishops showed no greater commitment to Latin America than their Anglo colleagues. In February 1990, when the Conference of Major Superiors of Men asked bishops to sign a petition to Congress demanding that the Administration revise its policy toward El Salvador in view of the murder of six Jesuits by the military and other acts of persecution of the church, the fifty bishops who signed included only three Hispanics: Archbishop Flores, Bishop Arturo Tafoya of the Diocese of Pueblo, and auxiliary Bishop Juan Arzube of Los Angeles. Flores no doubt raised unrealistic expectations with his performance in the first few years. Few of his peers, however, were willing or able to accept the risks he took. In later years even Flores was more circumspect. Age and illness had taken a toll. Asked about all this, he said that when he was first ordained bishop, he was all alone; now there are others who can speak out on the issues. But the younger bishops have not taken up his mantle.

As the new millennium began, the first generation of Hispanic bishops was, in the main, history. Moreover, the first generation of Hispanic bishops had largely passed from the scene. Patricio Flores, the only archbishop on the mainland, reached the mandatory retirement age of seventy-five in 2004 and his resignation was accepted by the end of that year. By then, most of the first twenty Hispanic bishops were no longer in office or were reaching retirement age. Alphonse Gallegos of Sacramento was killed in an auto accident. Rene Gracida, of Corpus Christi, and Enrique San Pedro, of Brownsville, Texas, died. Roberto Sanchez of Santa Fe, the only other archbishop, resigned in 1992. Others retired, among them Manuel Moreno of Tucson, Juan Arzube of Los Angeles, Rene Gracida of Corpus Christi, Agustín Román of Miami, and Francisco Garmendia of New York, who died in 2005. Joseph A. Madera, bishop of Fresno, had transferred to the military ordinariate after an investigation by the bishops of the finances of his diocese. By early 2006 he had retired.

Younger Hispanic bishops replaced them, but the first generation was missed because, in many of them, the spirit of the *Movimiento* blazed in their hearts. They knew that Hispanics could not advance unless they demanded change. They were outsiders with nothing to lose and therefore were not afraid to confront church and societal leaders. That fire burns less brightly in the second generation, in part because the *Movimiento*, at least in its willingness to confront, cooled down; in part because much has been accomplished; in part because the times call for a different strategy to seek change; but perhaps mainly because Hispanics are now fully accepted in the brotherhood of bishops.

In 2006 twenty-three Hispanic bishops were in office, ten of them serving as ordinaries, but only two as archbishops, the same number as twenty years previously. José A. Gómez, archbishop of San Antonio, replaced Flores in San Antonio in 2005. Roberto Gonzáles, a Puerto Rican, rose from auxiliary in Boston to the ordinary in Corpus Christi and now serves as the archbishop of San Juan, Puerto Rico. Ten others were listed as retired. In proportion to the Hispanic population, there should have been hundreds. Among the younger bishops ordained in recent years, two stood out: Gabino Zavala, auxiliary in the Archdiocese of Los Angeles, for his work with Pax Christi and as the chair of Encuentro 2000; and Jaime Soto, auxiliary in the Diocese of Orange, for being a strong defender of immigrants.

The Encuentro Movement

In September 1971 Father Robert Stern, director of the Hispanic Apostolate for the Archdiocese of New York, invited local leaders to meet with Father Edgard Beltran, formerly of the Latin American Episcopal Conference and then on the staff of the USCC's Division for the Spanish Speaking, to discuss a pastoral plan for Hispanic ministry. During the discussion Beltran said there ought to be a national *encuentro* (encounter) for Spanish-speaking leaders of the church of the United States. The proposal received widespread support and finally the blessing of Bishop Joseph L. Bernardin, general secretary of the United States Catholic Conference.

The First National Encuentro was held in June 1972 at Trinity College in Washington, D.C. It drew several hundred participants from across the nation. The common thread expressed by many at the meeting was that the church had to change from a policy of assimilation to one of pluralism. John Cardinal Krol, president of the National Conference of Catholic Bishops, tried to head off such thinking. He said:

> While in God's providence there are people of many different racial, ethnic, and national origins in our Church in the United States, and while each group has something distinctive and very precious to offer to the life of the total community out of its respective heritage, in the final analysis there is among us neither Jew nor Greek, neither

Irishman nor Pole, nor German, nor Italian, nor Anglo, nor Spanish speaking, nor black, nor white—but all of us are one in Christ Jesus, all are descendants of Abraham.[22]

Respectfully, but sometimes in rather blunt language, the Hispanics replied that that was not true. There were Anglos, and they were discriminating against Hispanics in the seminaries. There were Irishmen, and, though only 17 percent of the Catholics in the nation, they were represented by 56 percent of the bishops. There were Germans, and for a long time they had had bilingual and bicultural education in the Catholic schools. And there were bishops, but Hispanics were virtually excluded from their ranks.

As Bishop Flores put it:

From us have been stolen our lands, our language, our culture, our customs, our history and our way of religious expression. We have also been victims of oppression, discrimination, semi-slavery. We have been poorly paid for our work; we have lived in housing worse than that of monkeys in a zoo; we have not been admitted to some schools.[23]

In the face of all that, he charged, the church had been silent. That was the tone of many of the presentations. It was a time to air grievances stored over many generations. At the end, the delegates drew a list of seventy-eight conclusions and demands they were making of the church. They demanded many things that eventually came to pass: that the Division for the Spanish Speaking become a special office or secretariat; that more regional offices for Hispanics be established; that there be a Bishops' Committee for Hispanics; that more Hispanic bishops be named; that there be sections or special editions of diocesan newspapers in Spanish.

There were other demands, however, that would not be accepted: that basic Christian communities become a priority;

that women be ordained as deacons; that non-territorial parishes be established for Spanish speakers; that mature married
men be considered as possible candidates for the priesthood;
that the training of all candidates for the priesthood in all the
dioceses of the United States should include formation in spoken Spanish and Hispanic culture.

Archbishop Furey characterized the conclusions of the First
National Encuentro as the Magna Carta of Hispanic Catholics.
But other bishops were less enthusiastic. Sedillo said: "We do
not see the *encuentros* as a panacea. The whole idea is to create
an awareness of where the Spanish-speaking are in relation to
the local church and to show that the Church has in many instances neglected the needs of the Spanish-speaking."[24]

The *encuentro* led to a repetition of the process at the regional and, in some cases, diocesan levels. It was seen as an
opportunity for Hispanics to air their grievances. Sometimes
these were fierce confrontations that were not understood by
Anglo Catholics. Archbishop James V. Casey of Denver found
it necessary to explain in the *Denver Catholic Register* that the
archdiocese had not been pressured into holding the meeting:

> I want all of our people to understand that the questions
> raised at St. Thomas Seminary and the ensuing dialogue
> have happened because the Archdiocese of Denver issued
> the invitation for this to happen.
>
> The facilities of St. Thomas Seminary were gladly
> made available for the Encuentro for a two-day period.
> Bishop George Evans, Martin Work (a diocesan lay offi-
> cial), Father Hanifen and I went willingly to St. Thomas
> to listen and to learn, because the church of Denver is
> concerned.
>
> We were not besieged by the Chicano people nor were
> we forced in any way to have these two days of dialogue,
> but rather the Chicano people were there because we in-
> vited them to express openly, their ideas, thoughts and
> frustrations.[25]

In other areas the local or regional *encuentros* were less con-troversial, but they did give Hispanics the opportunity to voice their opinions about how the church ought to be responding to their needs. Though the National Conference of Catholic Bishops generally took a defensive posture when the conclu-sions were presented to it, it saw the *encuentros* as a useful pro-cess in dealing with the growing Hispanic minority. Five years later Hispanics, with approval of the NCCB, decided to hold another national *encuentro*.

The Second National Encuentro, held in Washington, D.C., in August 1977, represented a significant change. In the first one the participants, as envisioned by Beltran, had been the leaders—mostly clergy and religious plus a handful of bishops. For the second one, although thirty-four bishops attended, the laity had a much larger role. First, there was a grassroots con-sultation of about 100,000. The committee preparing the *encuentro* wanted to know from the people, members of Chris-tian communities and never before surveyed about their views, what their needs were and how the church could meet them. The results, organized at the diocesan and regional levels, were brought to Washington by the delegates. While only 250 people had attended the First National Encuentro, twelve hun-dred came to the second one, nearly five hundred as delegates and the rest as observers. Under the umbrella theme of evan-gelization, they discussed human rights, integral education, political responsibility and unity, and the challenge of pluralism. In contrast to the first meeting, there were no talks, except one by Archbishop Robert Sanchez explaining the process. The rest of the time was spent in workshops.

Forty-five conclusions came from the Second National Encuentro. Father Frank Ponce, assistant director of the Sec-retariat for Hispanics, synthesized them into five points. The delegates, he said, made a commitment to continue a process of reflection and growth in Christ as a Hispanic community. They resolved to form basic Christian communities, seeing that "it is here that future leaders are born and fostered." They resolved to correct injustices both inside and outside the church, especially those suffered by migrant farm workers, and undocumented immigrants. "The delegates clearly gave notice that Hispano culture can no longer be ignored in teaching the Catholic faith," Ponce said. Finally, as a common thread in all the documents, the delegates emphasized that lay ministers must be encouraged and recognized by the church.[26]

Unlike the First National Encuentro, the second was conducted entirely in Spanish. This gave an advantage to Cubans and other recent immigrants who knew the language well. At the same time, the Mexican Americans, who were more accustomed to English, became frustrated. For that reason they had less influence on the final outcome.

The delegates asked the church to be poor in spirit, to seek unity in diversity rather than in homogeneity, and to help eliminate economic disadvantage. They committed themselves to convert persons and structures in the church so as to return to the simplicity of the gospel message. Nevertheless, the conclusions were neither so concrete nor so prophetic as those of the First National Encuentro.

In 1983 the bishops approved the pastoral letter "The Hispanic Presence: Challenge and Commitment," which called Hispanics a blessing from God and authorized the Third National Encuentro. The process leading up to the meeting began with a door-to-door survey of persons alienated from the church. In Miami alone the energetic Cuban-dominated apostolate visited eleven thousand families. Afterward, most dioceses had their own *encuentro*, followed by regional meetings, and finally the Third National Encuentro held at Catholic University in 1985. Brazilian Father José Marins—who helped Latin America's feuding bishops achieve consensus at their conference in Puebla, Mexico, in 1979—facilitated the process. Now he played a similar role in unifying Hispanics in the United States around the broad outlines of a national pastoral plan for Hispanic ministry. The bishops finally approved the plan in 1987 but allocated no funds to implement it, leading some Hispanic leaders to compare it to a beautiful new car without wheels. But those dioceses most committed to Hispanic ministry, the most prominent being the Archdiocese of Los Angeles, implemented the plan with their own funds.

Not all Hispanic leaders were enthusiastic about the accomplishments of the *encuentros*. They suspected that the bishops embraced the movement because it provides high profile events that do not require a radical change in priorities. At a cost of $1 million every five to ten years, Hispanics can be pacified.[27] Nevertheless, there were gains, whether or not the bishops have implemented the conclusions. In going through the process of the Third National Encuentro, for example, many local leaders received invaluable training. Also, as mentioned above, instead of waiting for a national plan to come forth, some dioceses put their own plans into effect. Moreover, the *encuentros* made bishops more aware of the need to serve and respond to the Hispanic community.

Fifteen years after the Third National Encuentro, another large national meeting was held, Encuentro 2000, also led by the Secretariat for Hispanic Affairs. But the new director, Ronaldo Cruz, who had assumed that post after Pablo Sedillo retired, gave it a new orientation. It gathered representatives of the many cultures in the church so they could get to know one another's histories and aspirations and work together. His idea was that Hispanics should work to create a multicultural church.

Renewal

Long before the *encuentros*, the *Cursillo* (small course) had brought renewal to many American Catholics, both Anglo and Hispanic. An intense weekend experience of spiritual renewal, the *Cursillo* originated in Spain in 1947. Ten years later two Spanish pilots training at an air force base in Texas introduced it to Father Gabriel Fernández of Waco. Soon Fernández was conducting his own *Cursillo*.

Gaining quick acceptance, *Cursillo* was soon offered all over the country. It was given in both English and Spanish, with a directorate for each version in Dallas, Texas. By 1976 about 300,000 persons had made a *Cursillo,* including fifty to sixty bishops and about seven thousand priests and nuns. Unlike other movements, which fade after a time, it has continued to draw participants up to the present.

The *Cursillo* is a three-day program, experienced only once, of renewal and spiritual discipline. It combines charismatic and group-dynamics techniques with an emphasis on sacrifice, confession, and physical acts of penance. Many of the Hispanic leaders of the 1970s owed their social conscience to the *Cursillo,* including Cesar Chavez and many of the farm workers in his union.

The *Cursillo* also played an important role in the life of Patricio Flores. As an assistant at Holy Name Parish in Houston, where he spent his first seven years as a priest, Flores was forbidden to speak Spanish to Mexican American parishioners, even when they addressed him in that language. The pastor, Father John J. Cassata, later the bishop of Fort Worth, held that loyalty to the United States required that one speak English at all times, even in church. The *Cursillo* provided a needed outlet for Flores, if only for the opportunity to speak in Spanish. Traveling throughout Texas giving *Cursillos,* he gained the respect of many pastors who then recommended him to Archbishop Furey when he asked for nominations for bishop.

The movement was not initially accepted everywhere. While Flores was making his *Cursillo* in 1962, his own bishop, Wendelin J. Nold, was in Rome at the Vatican Council. Upon returning he banned the *Cursillo* in his diocese because he wanted nothing in Spanish, even though the council had replaced Latin with the vernacular for church services.[28] About a year later Nold reversed himself, seeing how effectively the *Cursillo* renewed the faith of Hispanics. He put Flores in charge.

Still, some bishops have continued to look with disfavor on the *Cursillo* in Spanish. For a time in the late 1970s Archbishop James V. Casey of Denver banned the *Cursillo* in Spanish, not, he claimed, because he objected to the language but because he thought that having it only in English would help bring Anglos and Hispanics together.

In 1976 only thirty-nine dioceses had a secretariat for *Cursillos* in Spanish. The directors, unhappy because they felt that many of their ideas, initiatives, and apostolic concerns clashed with those of the English secretariats, voted to establish their own national office. Only the concerted efforts of Bishop James Rausch, general secretary of the National Conference of Catholic Bishops, headed off the split.

Louis J. Reicher, ordinary of the Diocese of Austin, was the first bishop to give the *Cursillo* his approval, in 1959. By the middle of the 1970s the *Cursillo* was active in 120 of the 156 dioceses in the nation. In New York seventeen persons made it in 1958. By 1976 fourteen thousand Hispanics had taken part in *Cursillos* in Spanish. Quick to recognize its value, Francis Cardinal Spellman provided a meeting place. *Cursillos* in Spanish have been held continuously, but the English version was discontinued for a time. By 1976, 164 *Cursillos* had been given in New York for men and 125 for women, all in Spanish. The reception in Brooklyn was just as impressive.

Another movement imported from Spain was Marriage Encounter. This movement, founded by Father Gabriel Calvo, was brought to the United States in 1968 by sixty couples sponsored by the Christian Family Movement. When they arrived in Los Angeles, the chancery, suspicious of what the new movement would bring, did not want to provide them with an official forum. The sponsors finally found a place to meet in Soledad Parish in East Los Angeles. About the same time, Maryknoll Father Donald Hessler and a Mexican couple, Alfonso and Mercedes Gómez, led a Marriage Encounter at the University of Notre Dame. By 1973 more than seventeen thousand couples had experienced the weekend sessions intended to revitalize marriages. Three years later the movement had grown to seventy-seven thousand couples. An estimated sixty thousand people from Marriage Encounter groups throughout the nation gathered in Veterans Stadium in Philadelphia on August 2, 1976, for an evening liturgy during the Eucharistic Congress.[29]

Another movement, Movimiento Familiar Cristiano (MFC), is similar to the Christian Family Movement (CFM), but unlike the latter, which seems to have faded on a national level, it is still going. Originating in the 1960s like the CFM, the MFC has representation all over the country and is conducted in Spanish. About three thousand couples belonged to it in 1988. MFC, still strong in some regions, seeks to develop stronger families and better communities where people can live in harmony. It focuses first on marriage, then on the family and the community.

Basic Christian Communities

Organizing basic Christian communities (BCCs) was from the beginning a top priority of the Secretariat for Hispanics. After the chief promoter, Father Edgard Beltrán, became a layman and left his post, the impetus to organize BCCs came from parish and diocesan personnel.

In the Diocese of San Bernardino, Sister Rosa Marta Zárate began organizing BCCs among Hispanics in the 1970s, but some pastors opposed her work and, as a result, by 1988 Zárate was no longer working in the diocese. Similar problems occurred elsewhere. Griselda Velazco, a member of an interfaith community in Chicago, said her pastor told her, "I wish you much luck even though you will fail." Nevertheless, the group was so successful that it became a model for others. In the Archdiocese of Santa Fe a leadership-development team trained leaders for the BCCs; in San Diego, Bishop Chavez started an evangelization team that trained animators for the small communities. Though the laity has been enthusiastic, the BCCs have often lacked the episcopal support they enjoy in Latin America. The bishops as a group have been ambivalent. When communities were proposed by the First National Encuentro, the committee of bishops that examined the conclusions did not embrace the idea. But in their 1983 pastoral on Hispanics, the bishops called on the communities, along with other groups, to be a prophetic voice. The 1987 pastoral plan approved unanimously by the bishops made the communities a priority.

In recent years many local Hispanic apostolic ministries and movements have begun. In Miami, for example, Cuban lay people have instituted a dozen movements in Spanish, including the *Cursillo* and Family Encounter Movement; Camino al Matrimonio, a marriage-preparation movement; the Youth Encounter Movement; the confraternities of Our Lady of Charity; the Legion of Mary in Spanish; the Catholic University Group; and the charismatic movement in Spanish.

These initiatives have not always been welcomed. In the late 1970s Cubans felt that at least some church leaders did not see their apostolic movements as instruments of service. Monsignor Bryan O. Walsh, former episcopal vicar for the Spanish Speaking Peoples and Migrants, said, "Many of the difficulties but not all can be traced to what I would call a reluctant acceptance by the Church of cultural and language differences as a necessary evil during a limited period of adaptation."[30] In Miami and elsewhere the issue was whether and to what extent Hispanics would put their own stamp on the church.

Chapter 6

Ministers and Ministry

The church's paradigm of clerical ministry sees vocation as an individual choice, a man or woman called personally by God. It requires one to leave family and culture and become part of another community, the priesthood, brotherhood, or sisterhood, or, more specifically, the diocese, congregation, or religious community. When a man becomes a priest, he belongs to the bishop or religious superior, to whom he pledges allegiance and obedience. Only secondarily does he serve the family, nuclear and extended, and the community that ideally chose him for the religious life. The women must make a similar commitment. Clearly, Hispanics do not respond well to the demands of such a paradigm of vocation. In 2005 only 5 percent of all priests and 6 percent of all bishops were Hispanic 2,500 of 45,000 priests and 25 of 400 bishops), a proportion unchanged in twenty-five years. In the 1980s only 180 of the 1,400 Hispanic priests were native born.[1] The proportion among religious women was similar. Moreover, in 1997, only 4 percent of all ecclesial lay ministers were Hispanics. The causes are many.

For a long time Hispanics (as well as other minorities) were deemed unworthy. Church leaders often disparaged Hispanic belief, culture, religious practice, and lack of knowledge of the faith, clearly indicating to those interested in religious life that they were not qualified. More recently church leaders have seen

Hispanics as an asset; for example, in 1987 the bishops called Hispanics "a prophetic presence in the face of materialism and individualism in society."[2] Serious recruitment of men for the priesthood and women for religious life began only after the middle of the twentieth century and, even then, not by all bishops. Even after seminaries opened their doors, many pastors continued to discourage the few Hispanics who expressed interest in entering the seminary, and those who persevered were sometimes pushed out by their peers and by the faculty. Seeing no role models among the clergy, young men grew up thinking that the priesthood was not for them.

Those who persevered had to give up their heritage, cultural and religious, and embrace that of the majority. They were trained to serve the mainstream population rather than their own people, who were thus deprived of their service and example. Not surprisingly, Hispanic priests and sisters tended to emerge from formation with disdain for their own people and culture. When the civil rights movement of the 1960s and 1970s gave them new awareness of what they had surrendered, many rebelled and demanded to be assigned to serve their own people, whom they perceived as needing them more. Superiors responded as they usually do, causing some to leave religious orders or congregations, notably Jerry Barnes, now bishop of San Bernardino, who was denied ordination by a religious order, and Sister Petra Chavez, who had to resign from her congregation and begin anew with another one. Barnes went to San Antonio, where he found Archbishop Patricio Flores sympathetic to his needs. Others simply gave up their vocation and returned to the laity.

Service to one's own people is a powerful incentive. Hispanic ministers lead the fast-growing Hispanic evangelical churches. The Penitentes of New Mexico, the Spanish-speaking Cursillo, Marriage Encounter, and the Spanish charismatic movement have always had their own religious leaders. Parish-based organizations like Communities Organized for Public Service in San Antonio and similar groups in other large cities, all following the philosophy of the late Saul Alinsky, have developed many Hispanic leaders, who exercise their own special ministry to their communities. When there are no barriers, Hispanics, young and old alike, respond eagerly to the call to minister. When the late Bishop John Fitzpatrick of Brownsville invited applications for lay ministers in the diocese, 450 Hispanics applied. In New Mexico in the 1980s hundreds of people between the ages of ten and seventy made a one-hundred-mile pilgrimage for vocations annually, and hundreds more assisted the pilgrims along the way. That Spirit expresses itself in different ways in many areas.

Poor education, or lack of it, disqualifies many Hispanics, not only for the priesthood and religious life but also for lay positions in the chanceries and even in parishes. This is due to an outdated model of ministry in which the minister is, above all, supposed to be able to defend the faith. He is therefore trained to be an expert in theology, scripture, and related fields. Hispanics simply lack these prerequisites. According to 2000 Census data, only 57 percent of Hispanics had high school diplomas compared to 88 percent for non-Hispanic whites; only 11 percent twenty-five years of age or over had a bachelor's degree, compared to 28 percent of non-Hispanic whites. Because they often attend inferior schools, even those who graduate lack the qualifications to enter the seminary or a religious house of formation. Fewer yet possess the master's degree often required to apply for many lay positions, such as director of religious education. But in Denver, where the seminary found few candidates for a graduate program in Hispanic ministry, a deacon had numerous candidates in a parish program that did not require a high school or college education.

In the 1980s religious orders and some dioceses have started special houses of formation for Hispanics. Father Gary Riebe-Estrella, SVD, who headed a Hispanic-vocations project for the Bishops' Committee on Vocations, established a house of formation in the barrios of East Los Angeles, the model for others. In 1989 there were fourteen such houses in Los Angeles alone. They provided remedial education when needed, training in skills necessary for success in college, and cultural reinforcement that Hispanics often fail to find in the seminary. But few of the beneficiaries matriculated to seminaries. More recently, efforts have been made to make seminaries culturally friendly and to help educationally deprived candidates to meet educational requirements.

Poverty presents another obstacle. Hispanic families often cannot afford the tuition and other expenses for a seminary education. Because they must contribute economically to the support of the family, many young men and women drop out of high school or college to go to work. Having to pay their own expenses, as required by some dioceses, also deters some from ministry as permanent deacons. Others encounter problems after ordination. In a parish in Denver, a Hispanic who worked as a janitor was not allowed to preach. In Omaha, the author, a non-deacon, was invited to give the homily at Masses in English and Spanish, but the ordained deacon in the parish was not. In part, it is the idea that only the highly educated can speak about the gospel, but even the learned have problems, as illustrated by the experience of Antonio Sandoval. Ordained a deacon in 1973 while working as a tenured chemistry professor at the University of Missouri in Kansas City, he served one year as a missionary in Belize and then, in 1980, came to Colorado to devote himself full time to Hispanic ministry.

Since deacons in the Archdiocese of Denver received no pay, Sandoval established a missionary society to support his work and the assistants he recruited. He was like an old-time circuit rider, going between Denver and Burlington on the Kansas border, 180 miles away, preaching in half a dozen or more parishes. He founded Bible-study and prayer groups, went door to door to bring people back to the faith, gave several talks each week on the scripture of the Sunday Mass, and worked with migrant workers who had no one to serve them. But when Archbishop J. Francis Stafford became the ordinary of Denver in 1986, he asked Sandoval to dissolve the missionary society, although a board of priests and sisters directed its activity.

Sandoval reincorporated as a nonprofit educational society to be able to continue serving the migrants and worked in a parish. But when that assignment ended after three years, the archdiocese refused to give him an assignment for the next eleven years. He supported his family and educated his children by adjunct teaching and running science and drug education programs in the public schools, never giving up the hope to be incardinated. That finally happened in 1999 when the priest in charge of the diaconate program died. That day a priest friend called: "The king has died; if you apply, you will get your diaconate license now." He succeeded but had to work without compensation at his home parish, St. Augustine, Brighton, Colorado. In 2006, however, Sandoval, seventy-five, was a salaried deacon at Our Lady Mother of the Church in Commerce City, Colorado, describing it as the best assignment he ever had.

In part, at least, similar resistance explains why there are so few editors and writers in the Catholic press, another aspect of the prejudice deeming them unworthy. The mastheads of newspapers and magazines show Hispanics only in circulation and promotion, and then only a few. To read some Catholic papers in dioceses where Hispanics are nearly or already the majority, one would think that their proportion is much lower. The Archdiocese of Los Angeles, however, has a separate diocesan newspaper in Spanish, as does the Archdiocese of Miami. The only publications Hispanics head, and not always, are Spanish-language editions or sections of diocesan newspapers.

In the 1980s faculties of Catholic universities and seminaries had few Hispanic professors, a deficiency due in part to the lack of priests and nuns and to the small percentage of Hispanics with advanced academic degrees. Few Hispanics sat on church boards and commissions or participated in the peace and refugee movements. Twenty years later there were a few more but hardly in proportion to the growing Hispanic population.

Hispanic pastoral centers like the Mexican American Cultural Center (MACC), the Southeast Pastoral Institute in Miami, and regional offices for Hispanic ministry, could never count on having funds for future operations. They depended on the transient largesse of dioceses, foundations, and religious orders. Their efforts to develop support among the beneficiaries of their programs had been only marginally successful; for example, MACC raised only about half of its annual budget in the 1980s.

"1 just hope that to continue having MACC all of us who have benefited from it will contribute, especially in a financial way," said Bishop Ricardo Ramírez, who served as vice president of the center for several years. "We cannot be beggars all our lives, on the receiving end all the time. We must not only own it because we feel good about MACC. We must dish out."[3] The American Board of Catholic Missions was generous toward pastoral centers like MACC, but drastic cuts sometimes occurred. The bishops, however, have been loathe to provide special help. While allowing a national collection for black Catholics, the bishops have refused to do the same for Hispanics. Nonetheless, MACC and pastoral centers like the Southeast Pastoral Institute for Hispanics in Miami endured and were still in operation in 2005.

The Church's Special Service to Hispanics

By establishing the Bishops' Committee for the Spanish Speaking in 1945, the church recognized that Hispanics had special needs that were not being met through its traditional apostolates. But the programs started by the committee, while meeting some spiritual and social needs, also served other interests. One concern was to frustrate Protestant proselytizing.

Another was Americanization, through which the church enhanced its status in society.

But at no time was that special service to Hispanics more than a secondary mission. The bishops were at all times careful not to jeopardize the support of the Anglo community, which was the primary source of vocations, status, and funds. For that reason they were slow to oppose the abuses of the *bracero* program. Naively, the bishops thought they could achieve their goal of bettering the lives of farm workers without antagonizing growers. At one point Father James L. Vizzard, SJ, head of the Catholic Rural Life Conference, declared:

> Church authorities often are frozen with fear that if they take a stand with the workers the growers will punish them in the pocketbook. . . . Church institutions do not exist for their own sake. Nor does the Church itself exist solely for the comfortable, affluent, and powerful who support those institutions. Christ had a word to say about the shepherd who, out of fear and because the sheep weren't his, abandoned the sheep when they were under attack.[4]

In 1950 the bishops' committee staff sought to improve low farm wages by consulting Catholic landowners in the Rio Grande Valley who, according to the staff, were "ready and willing to work out a just wage system." The committee thought the example and influence of Catholic growers would influence those who sought "to keep the laboring masses in wage slavery."[5] In the Diocese of Green Bay the priest running the program for farm workers, while recognizing the need to speak out unequivocally for social justice whenever conscience required, urged moderation to keep the goodwill of the growers.[6] The allocation of funds revealed how peripheral Hispanics were. The American Board of Catholic Missions gave $1.3

million to the church in Texas from 1925 to 1951. Of that, $980,000 was spent in Anglo parishes and only $390,000 in Hispanic parishes—even though two out of every three Catholics in the state were Hispanics.[7]

While the service carried out under the auspices of the bishops' committee was an important step in terms of the magnitude of the needs, it remained at best a gesture. In Arkansas a 1956 survey revealed that there was only one Spanish-speaking priest to minister to thirty thousand *braceros*. The previous year there had been none.[8] In 1953 the bishops' committee brought in twenty-four Mexican priests to work in dioceses with the most *braceros*. They worked as far north as Michigan and Idaho, and the dioceses participating expressed satisfaction with the arrangement. But the program did not endure.

The Catholic Councils for the Spanish Speaking, created by the bishops' committee in 1945, fulfilled an advisory role. While the committee functioned in four episcopal provinces, the councils soon spread beyond. States with Hispanic agricultural workers soon had their own councils. As time went on, the councils were organized in Missouri, the upper Pacific Coast, Montana, and the upper Midwest. By the 1960s, with Puerto Rican farm workers in states along the Eastern seaboard, there were councils in that region.

The councils were made up of a representative of the local bishop and other priests and lay people, including members of Catholic Action, the Confraternity of Christian Doctrine, women religious, school officials, the director of Catholic Charities, members of doctors' and lawyers' guilds, and so forth. The councils fulfilled an important educational and social function. Perhaps for the first time in the experience of many of their members, Anglo and Hispanic Catholics sat down together to address common problems. Lack of contact has long been a problem between the two communities. The councils, trying to address that problem, included Spanish-speaking members whenever possible. The councils strongly opposed the inflow of illegal immigrants. Father Raymond

McGowan of the National Catholic Welfare Conference said: "The Catholic Council fights this invasion. It fights also for laws and unions to protect domestic farm labor on the commercial farms. It fights for laws, federal and state, to protect unions, wages, hours, and security in non-factory jobs . . . jobs which escape . . . the protection of nearly all labor law."[9]

Such eloquent rhetoric was rarely matched by effective action, but the councils did provide a forum to begin building awareness of the problems. They sponsored annual conferences that drew an increasing number of participants and focused attention on pressing social issues. At the conference in 1962 there were representatives from twenty-six states as well as Mexico, Puerto Rico, and Cuba. A reorganization leading to the creation of the National Office for the Spanish Speaking deprived the councils of a national role, but many continued to meet on a diocesan basis.

The model demonstrated by those early efforts has not changed much in the subsequent sixty years. Hispanic ministry is still considered as service to a population largely passive. In that respect, it has improved in many ways. Thousands of religious men and women have been trained at centers such as MACC and the Southeast Pastoral Institute in Miami. Many seminarians are required to learn some Spanish in order to be ordained, and many bishops can give at least a halting homily in Spanish. Special offices for Hispanic ministry have sprung up in most dioceses.

Efforts to Integrate Two Churches

Puerto Ricans who moved into the cities after World War II had a particularly difficult time practicing their faith. By then church policy had changed on national parishes. Other ethnic groups who had arrived previously had enjoyed a long period of adjustment during which strong community ties had been cemented through the parish. The Puerto Ricans, however, had no such opportunity. They were immediately forced to go to parishes where they were not wanted. While church leaders may have looked upon the process as integration, the reality was different. The Hispanics were kept apart in various ways. Encarnación Armas, a long-time leader and spokesperson for Puerto Ricans, said her people had to attend Mass in the basement—and they had to file through the alley to get there.[10]

In Brighton, Colorado, where the author lived, Hispanics were welcome only at the nine o'clock Mass every Sunday. If they went to any other Mass, they received hostile looks and sometimes were told outright to stay away. In towns in the Southwest that had one church for Anglos and another for Hispanics, life continued as usual. Integration did not occur until much later. At the First National Encuentro in Washington in 1972, then-Bishop Patricio Flores said that although the signs "No Mexicans allowed" had been removed, the attitudes of rejection remained. In some places where migrant workers were occasionally allowed to use the parish hall, the building was fumigated immediately afterward.

Ministry was poor because the clergy spoke no Spanish and had no respect for Hispanic culture. The Archdiocese of New York was among the few that tried to correct the problems. Its Institute of Cultural Communication, founded in 1957, sent priests to Puerto Rico, the Dominican Republic, and Colombia to study language and culture. By the end of the 1970s, about six hundred priests and two hundred nuns knew at least some Spanish.[11] Unfortunately, many other dioceses did not have a similar program.

Integration of the Catholic schools was more difficult. In some areas Anglos withdrew their children when Hispanics were admitted. In others integration did not occur because Hispanics lived in segregated neighborhoods. Nationally, only 5 percent of Catholic school enrollment was Hispanic in the 1970s. In some cities, like Chicago, Los Angeles, and New York, the breakdown was better. In 1979, in the Archdiocese of New York, 22 percent of the elementary students and 20 percent of those in high school were Hispanic.[12] In Brooklyn and Newark, the percentages were 15.3 and 13.5, respectively. But, at the same time, Hispanics were more than half the Catholics in the Archdiocese of New York and 40 percent of those in Brooklyn. Hispanics, therefore, were still under-represented.

In other areas only token integration occurred. In Philadelphia, where 100,000 Puerto Ricans lived, only 0.5 percent of the Catholic school students were Hispanic. In Washington, D.C., another city with a large Hispanic community, only 3.6 percent of Hispanic children were in Catholic schools. Generally, policy of the bishops aside, pastors did not expend great energy in creating one community out of their flock. In Colorado in the 1960s pastors sometimes refused to witness marriages between Anglos and Hispanics. Even after Vatican II, some continued to refuse to offer Mass in Spanish. In New Mexico in the mid-1970s a pastor in an Albuquerque suburb refused to allow a Mass in Spanish in a parish where 98 percent of the members were Hispanics. But he faithfully offered a Mass in Polish.

The *Movimiento*

The Hispanic movement for civil rights, also called the Chicano movement because of the name the activists chose to identify themselves, challenged the church to respect culture and religious traditions and work for social justice. Unlike the black movement for civil rights, which was led by ministers, the Hispanic counterpart was led largely by lay persons. Hispanics were appalled at the hypocrisy they saw in their church. On the one hand, they heard bishops and clergy asking them to adopt the trappings of American life. But when it came to demanding the rights that gave meaning to being an American, they found themselves counseled in patience and acceptance of an unjust status quo. For this reason the church itself became one target of the *Movimiento*.

Hispanics demanded that the church accept their language and culture. They further asked the church to involve itself in the struggle of the poor for a more human life. It galled farm workers that only non-Catholics, members of the Migrant Ministry of the National Council of Churches and Jewish leaders, walked alongside them on the picket lines in the vineyards of California. They were even more upset at the silence of the church on key issues. "We have been victims of oppression, discrimination, semi-slavery, poorly paid for our work," Bishop Flores said at the First National Encuentro in 1972. "We have lived in conditions sometimes worse than the animals in the zoo. And yet the Church keeps silent."[13]

In fact, the church was not totally silent about the injustices. But its statements aimed to please all sides. The bishop of Monterey-Fresno said the church supported the theories and concepts of social justice but did not align itself with "a particular union, owner organization, or other secular enterprise."[14] Bishop Humberto Medeiros of Brownsville defended union organization but in the same breath spoke of the right of "any other group of men who need to unite in order to protect and defend against the unjust demands of management or labor.[15] In 1949 four priests of the Archdiocese of San Francisco organized the Mission Band to serve farm workers in California. Fathers Thomas McCullough, Donald McDonnell, John García, and Ronald Burke convinced Archbishop John J. Mitty that the church was not serving the hundreds of thousands of farm workers in the state. Aspiring to be priests of the poor, they traveled up and down the valleys of California for twelve years.

As part of their ministry, they made farm workers aware of the social doctrine of the church and of their rights as workers. One of the leaders who benefited was Cesar Chavez, principal organizer of the United Farm Workers Union. He spent many nights discussing with Father McDonnell the teachings on the rights of labor. The education was mutual, because the missioners also became aware of the injustices suffered by the workers.

The work of these priests brought into play the fundamental dilemma the church always faces: support of the poor brings confrontation with the rich. The growers soon began to question the right of the four priests to speak for the church. In 1958 the growers, realizing they could not intimidate Mitty, started to pressure other bishops in California. They accused the priests of meddling in politics and suggested that the church should not be exempt from taxation. In 1958 and 1959 many growers in the Stockton area sent the local bishop a signed statement to the effect that, unless he pulled the priests out, "the Church should be registered as a lobbyist and denied tax-free status."[16] As a result, the bishop of the Diocese of Fresno, Aloysius J. Willinger, denounced the priests of the Mission Band as leftists following the communist line. The bishop of San Diego, Charles F. Buddy, declared that it was not the proper role of the Mission Band to help the farm workers organize to win social justice.

Mitty never gave in, but when he was terminally ill, in 1962, the chancellor of the Archdiocese of San Francisco ended the Mission Band. The four priests were ordered to avoid further involvement in agricultural labor. Nevertheless, the Mission Band established a pattern of service that was to be emulated in other areas.

In Texas, when organizing activity began in 1966, two "outside" priests came to assist the workers: Father William Killian, executive director of the San Antonio archdiocesan weekly, and Father Sherrill Smith, social action director for the Archdiocese of San Antonio. As in California, the growers called them intruders who did not speak for the church. Bishop Medeiros of Brownsville asked Archbishop Lucey of San Antonio to withdraw them. Killian and Smith were ordered out in 1967. Lucey sent them to New Mexico on a mandatory retreat and suspended four other priests who protested his action publicly.[17]

Protestants also forced the bishops to act. When Chavez and the farm workers were finally able to go on strike in 1965 after Congress canceled the *bracero* program, the California Migrant

Ministry was the first church presence in the camps. Chavez asked: "Why do the Protestants come out here and help the people, demanding nothing and give all their time to serving the farm workers, while our own parish priests stay in their churches where few people come and feel uncomfortable?"[18] In response, Bishop Timothy Manning of Fresno appointed Father Mark Day chaplain of the farm workers.

The person most responsible for winning church support was Cesar Chavez, himself. First, there was the unselfish witness of his personal life. While leaders of other unions received huge salaries, he lived on five dollars a week plus expenses, just like any other member of the union. He refused offers of well-salaried positions. He made sacrifice a reality in his own life. He emphasized that when a person sacrifices, he forces others to do the same:

> When we are really honest with ourselves we must admit that our lives are all that really belong to us. So it is how we use our life that determines what kind of men we are. It is my deepest belief that only by giving our lives do we find life. I am convinced that the truest test of courage, the strongest act of manliness is to sacrifice ourselves for others in totally non-violent struggle for justice. To be a man is to suffer for others. God help us to be men.[19]

Second, Chavez organized the church behind him by using religious symbols in his struggle. When the farm workers marched hundreds of miles to Sacramento to present their grievances to the state legislature, the banner of Our Lady of Guadalupe led the marchers. In 1968 he made a twenty-five day fast for peace and nonviolence, during which he lost thirty-five pounds. By the end he was almost too weak to walk or talk.

But it was Chavez's commitment to nonviolence, the strongest feature of his spirituality, that finally swung the bishops, cautious as always, behind him. Chavez cultivated two ideals: the nonviolence of Jesus and the spirit of Saint Francis of Assisi.

He believed that the poor could be more powerful than the wealthy because there was nothing anyone could take from them.

In 1969 the National Conference of Catholic Bishops refused to support the international grape boycott. But it appointed an Ad Hoc Committee on Farm Labor: Bishop Joseph F. Donnelly of Hartford, chairman; Bishop Medeiros of Brownsville; Bishop Hugh Donohue of Fresno; and Bishop Walter Curtis of Bridgeport, Connecticut. Monsignor George Higgins of the United States Catholic Conference was named consultant to the committee and Monsignor Roger Mahony its secretary.[20]

Thanks to the mediation of the committee, within six months the United Farm Workers had nearly one hundred contracts with grape growers. Then the bishops mediated a jurisdictional dispute with the Teamsters Union in the lettuce fields. But the growers and Teamster locals refused to abide by the agreements. Three years later the grape growers refused to renegotiate with the UFW and the workers went out on strike again.

During the summer of 1973 the police arrested four thousand persons, including sixty priests and religious. The protestors were challenging court injunctions they saw as prejudicial and unconstitutional. Many strikers, men and women, were beaten. On August 1 a shotgun blast from a passing truck wounded an eighteen-year-old man picketing at the Tudor ranch in Tulare County. Ten days later shots fired from a field in the Missakian vineyards near Delano wounded Marcelina Barajas and Paul Salgado. The same day a car driven by a private policeman struck three pickets in Kern County. On August 16 a sniper shot sixty-year-old Juan de La Cruz dead as he and his wife stood on the picket line at the Giumara vineyards. Two days later Nagi Mohsin Daifullah died after a deputy struck him on the head with a flashlight. In the face of such violence Chavez suspended picketing and instituted a grape boycott that eventually brought the growers to the bargaining table again.

In the period between its creation in 1969 and 1973 the Bishops' Committee on Farm Labor shed its neutrality. In 1973 Bishop Donnelly and Monsignor Higgins stood on the picket line with the farm workers when growers in the Coachella Valley refused to sign new contracts. They were influenced by a decision of the California Supreme Court that the Teamsters had been in collusion with lettuce growers and by an attempt to pass Proposition 22, which was, in the words of Father Eugene Boyle of the National Federation of Priests Councils, "extremely disenfranchising of the poor."[21] As a result of all this, the bishops voted to support the farm workers' lettuce and grape boycotts. The issue seemed to have been settled when the California legislature passed the Agricultural Labor Relations Act in 1975.

Bishop Roger Mahony, recently promoted to auxiliary bishop of Fresno, headed the board appointed to mediate labor disputes. For a time, under a Democrat governor in Sacramento, the law worked well. But in the 1980s a Republican governor, George Deukmejian, and a less sympathetic legislature cut funding and the Act was poorly administered or not at all. The contracts of the UFW dwindled and unfavorable judgments in two lawsuits put financial strains on the union. Union membership went from fifty thousand in 1970 to fifteen thousand in the mid-1980s. Chavez instituted a new grape boycott, but the public responded poorly. In 1988 Chavez underwent another long fast, which stirred only transient sympathy and commitment, leaving the future of the UFW in doubt. He died unexpectedly one spring night in 1993 after testifying all day in a lawsuit by a grower whose lettuce was boycotted by the UFW. Arturo Rodríguez, Chavez's son-in-law, became president of the union, settled the legal challenges, and increased union membership. But the farm workers remained among the lowest-paid workers in the nation, their health at risk from dangerous pesticides.

Farm-worker organizing had been even less successful in other states. In Arizona a right-to-work law blocked union organizing. In Texas the violence of the Texas Rangers and other police forces and unconstitutional acts sanctioned by the courts defeated the farm workers. In 1975 a melon grower, C. I. Miller of Hidalgo County, fired an automatic shotgun at striking workers, wounding eleven. Though he boasted publicly that he had "opened season" on them, a grand jury refused to indict him. Legislatures had not passed a law similar to the California Act, nor had Congress modified labor law to include farm workers. This sad condition was due to the political power of the growers and the indifference of the legislators.

Urban Struggles

The church in the 1970s also became involved in the urban struggle of Hispanics, but in a less public way. Often only Hispanic clergy participated. New Mexico priests joined the marches and meetings of the Alianza Land Grants Movement of northern New Mexico. They also helped packinghouse workers in Albuquerque win better pay and working conditions, joined a coalition of Concerned Citizens for Better Education, and pushed for an end to discrimination in the judicial system in New Mexico. In Denver, bishops and priests were ambivalent about the Crusade for Justice, founded in 1965 by a former high-ranking boxer turned politician, poet, and, ultimately barrio leader, Rodolfo Corky González. The Crusade for Justice struggled against the dehumanization of urban life: schools with a semblance of jails, policemen who brutalized both innocent and the guilty, businesses owned by outsiders that gouged residents of the barrios, and other forms of discrimination. The Crusade for Justice supported students who walked out of schools protesting the remarks of a teacher who said Mexicans were stupid. Because González, unlike Cesar Chavez, did not espouse nonviolence, the church was cautious. Nevertheless, the archdiocese provided aid to the Crusade's Tlatelolco School, which sought to instill Hispanic values and culture, both denigrated in the city's schools. One year Archbishop James Casey came unannounced to the Crusade's Easter Mexican dinner, donated one-hundred dollars to the building fund, and urged those present to cherish their history and culture.

The most significant urban issue in which the church played a crucial role was the strike that began on May 10, 1972, at the Farah Manufacturing Company. At that time Farah was the largest manufacturer of men's slacks in the nation, with plants in Albuquerque and Las Cruces in New Mexico and in El Paso, Victoria, and San Antonio in Texas. The company president, William Farah, would not recognize the union the workers had elected to represent them. There were 10,400 employees, 85 percent of them Mexican American women earning an average weekly salary of sixty-nine dollars. After the workers consulted with El Paso's Bishop Sydney Metzger, he became their chief advocate. When the strikers instituted a boycott of Farah slacks and jeans, Metzger wrote to every Catholic bishop in the country, expressing his support of the strike and endorsing the boycott.

With Metzger's support a Mexican American priest, Jesse Muñoz, made his parish the headquarters of the strike. On Tuesday afternoons the strikers had their weekly meeting at the church. Weekly strike benefits and special relief checks for workers from Juarez, across the Rio Grande from El Paso, were passed out at the parish hall. Another priest, Donald Bauer, worked full time with the union, the Amalgamated Clothing Workers of America. The Chamber of Commerce, the business community, and the local press vilified Metzger and Muñoz. Some Protestant clergy campaigned for Farah, but the Texas Conference of Churches endorsed the strike. Its efforts—and those of other bishops and Catholic clergy—helped cause a $10 million drop in sales for Farah in 1972 and another $10 million in 1973. The stock of the manufacturer fell from thirty dollars to eight dollars a share. Farah closed plants and dismissed workers wholesale, but after twenty-one months the union won its struggle.

A more far-reaching service of the church to Hispanic urban areas was carried out through the Campaign for Human Development (CHD), the church's anti-poverty program, begun in 1970. The CHD contributed to many self-help projects or causes that made a significant difference in the lives of Hispanics. For example, in 1971 it gave $100,000 to PADRES to develop a mobile ministry team. In 1977 it gave a grant to the Mexican American Legal Defense and Educational Fund to seek voting rights for disenfranchised Mexican Americans. During that same period it helped Communities Organized for Public Service (COPS) to get started in San Antonio.

By the beginning of the twenty-first century, in public life and in the church, the *Movimiento* was history. The Chicano generation aged, mellowed, settled for the gains it had achieved, or simply passed from the scene. It was replaced by people with a different history, as demonstrated by statistics from California. In 1980, eight in ten Hispanics were native born; in 1995, two-thirds of all Hispanics in Los Angeles County were foreign born.[22] What's more, the Hispanic population is more diversified, having integrated hundreds of thousands who came from Central America in the 1980s. This new generation says it is concerned about social issues but will address them in its own way. And perhaps more significant in terms of ministry, as Hispanics became more than one-third of California's population they were more concerned with renewing a mainstream society in decline than in preserving a minority movement.

Communities Organized for Public Service

COPS began in 1973 when Ernesto Cortés, a native of San Antonio's West Side slums, fresh from training at Saul Alinsky's

Industrial Areas Foundation in Chicago, began knocking on doors looking for leaders with a following and with a network of communication. He found both in the parishes and among the presidents of the Holy Name Society, the Ladies Guild or school PTAs. Soon, too, the pastors and curates became involved. A tall, blunt young priest, Al Benavides, became the chief spokesperson for COPS, a federation of thirty-eight organizations from Catholic parishes and a scattering of Protestant churches based in the inner-city barrios of San Antonio. COPS helped change the election system from at large to single district for city councilors. As a result, poor areas won political power they had previously lacked. Long neglected by city and county government, they soon won $100 million in needed improvements, such as storm drains, adequate water and sewers, street paving, and traffic lights at dangerous intersections. At the group's first annual convention, Bishop Patricio Flores told them:

> You are here today not as supplicants with downcast eyes, not as welfare recipients, not as beggars. You are here as equals, as responsible law-abiding, tax-paying people. You are a people who with your sweat have helped shape this country, this state and particularly this city. You seek no special favor. You seek a just share of your tax monies to have a decent community. You have a right to equal and just consideration.[23]

When he saw what COPS had accomplished for the poor in San Antonio, Bishop Juan Arzube urged the CHD to fund a similar group in East Los Angeles. There was opposition from Catholic Charities, and a strong in-house battle ensued, finally decided in Arzube's favor by Cardinal Timothy Manning. Soon afterward, Ernie Cortés began organizing and, in time, United Neighborhoods Organization was achieving impressive results. After Cortés had finished there, he moved on to Houston. Others began similar organizations in El Paso and in the Rio

Grande Valley in Texas. In the process of revitalizing the community, COPS did the same for the participating parishes. At St. Timothy's, where Father Benavides was the pastor, Sunday Mass attendance went from seven hundred to thirteen hundred each Sunday. Lay leaders trained by COPS were soon improving and adding to the services offered by the parish: a new catechetical program, services to the elderly, a new liturgy that drew a citywide congregation. Social involvement, rather than conflicting with spiritual concerns, enhanced all aspects of the parish's programs.

Theology

The history of Hispanic theology begins with Father Félix Varela (1788–1853), a Cuban exile who spent many years doing pastoral work among poor Irish immigrants in New York City and served as vicar general of the Archdiocese of New York. He wrote a political theology titled *Letters to Elpidio*, in which he sought to integrate faith and the cause of liberty. His theological context, that of a patriot seeking independence for Cuba from Spain, was similar to that of modern Hispanic theologians in the United States whose theology is rooted in the social, economic, political, cultural, and pastoral life their people.

The modern pioneer of Hispanic theology, Father Virgil Elizondo, focused on *mestizaje,* the blending of races, as a theological gateway to understanding the historical experience of Hispanics in the United States. He also wrote about Our Lady of Guadalupe as the myth allowing access to the heart of Mexican and Mexican American culture and identity. Between 1960 and 1980 he was the only prominent US Hispanic theologian, gaining wide acclaim for his reflections on religion and culture and lecturing all over the world on his theology of *mestizaje.*

Gradually Elizondo was joined by others. In 1988 Father Allan Figueroa Deck, SJ, and Father Arturo Bañuelas, a diocesan priest from El Paso, founded the Academy of Catholic Hispanic Theologians of the United States (ACHTUS). By mid-1989 it had identified eighty Hispanics eligible for membership. Forty of them joined, and many others followed. They were strongly encouraged by Latin America's most eminent theologians, among them Gustavo Gutiérrez, Juan Luis Segundo, Enrique Dussel, Jon Sobrino, and Leonardo Boff. They urged US Hispanics to develop their own theology out of their own historical experience rather than simply adapting Latin America's.

Over the years, the members of ACHTUS have written and published extensively on culture, popular religion, spirituality, liturgy, feminism, and *mestizaje*. Some of them won advanced degrees at prestigious divinity schools like Harvard, Princeton, and the Institut Catholique in Paris. In 2004 Orbis Books, publisher of many of these works, received the academy's annual Virgil Elizondo Award for "outstanding contributions to a theology of and for Hispanics."

Hispanic theologians describe themselves as a bridge between the First World and the Third World, yet not being in either one; between North American feminism and the theological achievements of women in Latin America; and between the different analytical tools used in the United States and Latin America to analyze reality, the first step in constructing a theology.

Other Developments

In the 1990s a group led by Jesuit Father Allan Figueroa Deck organized the National Catholic Council for Hispanic Ministry, which seeks to strengthen the commitment of Hispanics, both youth and adults, to serve in the church as well as in politics, business, labor, and the media. Every few years the council has a national conference for Hispanic Catholic leaders in all these areas. With foundation funding the council has sponsored various training programs for Hispanic leadership. A guiding premise of the council is that know-how and training will involve more Hispanics in ministry.

The charismatic movement also revitalized the spiritual life of many Hispanics. There were hundreds of Spanish-speaking prayer groups throughout the country. In the Archdiocese of Los Angeles alone an estimated sixty thousand people belonged to the movement, most of them of Mexican origin. Many were associated with Charisma in Missions, led by Marilynn Kramer, a former Assembly of God minister who became a convert to Catholicism. She said that Charisma in Missions touched the lives of more than a half million people each year.[24] Hispanics found in the movement the warmth they experienced in their popular religion. Though Los Angeles undoubtedly led, the charismatic renewal was strong in many other areas. It has been credited with keeping many Hispanics in the Catholic Church who might otherwise have joined Protestant denominations.

There were many developments in liturgy. The Instituto de Liturgia Hispana was organized at the MACC in the late seventies at the urging of Jesuit Father John Gallen. By 1989 it had a membership of about one hundred. It assisted the Bishops' Committee on the Liturgy in its work. A Subcommittee on Hispanic Liturgy, headed in 1989 by Bishop Ricardo Ramírez, adapted many official texts for Spanish liturgy. The Northeast Pastoral Center put together the first Spanish-language lectionary for use by Spanish speakers in the United States.

Conclusion

For many years to come ministry by Hispanics will continue to be, as it has been during the last fifty years, a collective endeavor. Movements like the *Cursillo* and the *encuentros* of the 1970s and 1980s are the models. Just as the *Cursillo* revitalized the faith of all Catholics, the *encuentros* crafted the national pastoral plan for Hispanic ministry approved by the bishops in 1987. The process brought together Hispanic ecclesial and community leaders—priests, sisters, lay leaders, farm workers, and people alienated from the church—and together they crafted a *pastoral de conjunto* (collective ministry) that depends not on individual leaders as much as on the community. It is the ministry of organized farm workers, immigrants, poor urban dwellers. Collectively, they are changing the church and society.

Hispanic ministry began by efforts of the church to serve a population seen only as its objects. In the next stage Hispanics in ministry demanded assignment to serve their own people. Then came the concept of ministry by groups or special institutions established for that purpose. By the new millennium leaders were beginning to direct their efforts to serving the entire church, one increasingly multicultural. But all along a more powerful model has been at work: the ministry of the community as a whole, operating in the church and in society, without barriers or credentials, to revitalize the society in the world's richest nation. This is a silent ministry, that of the refugees who have endured persecution; the parents who dare to have children in an age of fear and insecurity; the poor, exploited immigrants who send millions to support their families in the home country; the poor who have not lost their ability to celebrate in the midst of deprivation. Then there is the ministry of the Latin American churches to the US church as a whole, bringing the wisdom of Medellín and Puebla, the experience of basic Christian communities in Brazil and elsewhere, and the teaching of its theologians. In all these aspects Hispanic ministry is flourishing.

Chapter 7

The Church and Immigrants

In 1922 the US bishops established an office in El Paso to help the many Mexicans forced to immigrate during the Mexican Revolution and its aftermath. It was not, however, the start of a strong corporate church commitment to Mexican immigrants, as demonstrated by the church's silence during the mass deportations of immigrants as well as citizens during the Great Depression. Nevertheless, migrations of Mexicans and other Latinos continued to challenge the church throughout the twentieth century and into the twenty-first: in the 1940s and 1950s of Puerto Ricans, who were not foreigners but citizens; then the Cuban exodus after Fidel Castro overthrew the dictator Fulgencio Batista in 1959; followed in the 1970s and 1980s by Central and South Americans fleeing wars by military regimes supported by the United States; and, in every decade, a new migration of Mexicans, the vast majority of the estimated ten million undocumented immigrants in the nation in 2005.[1]

The Puerto Rican Migration

Between 1950 and 1960 the Puerto Rican population living on the mainland went from 300,000 to 887,000. By 1970 it had increased to 1.4 million people of Puerto Rican birth or parentage. The exodus was so great that it was comparable to fifty million people leaving the United States to settle elsewhere. It affected most families. One cause was the decline of agriculture in Puerto Rico. From 1940 to 1970 the number of farm jobs dropped from 230,000 to 74,000.[2] Moreover, society offered little opportunity for upward mobility. Real unemployment was several times higher than on the mainland; in 1970 it was nearly 30 percent.[3] The mainland offered more job opportunities at better pay. But in times of recession in the United States, as in the early 1970s, the migration actually reversed.

The Puerto Ricans are poorer than any other Hispanic group in the nation; in 1986 their family income was twelve thousand dollars less than that of Cubans, the wealthiest Hispanic group, and five thousand dollars less than that of Mexican Americans. Puerto Rican median family income was $14,584 as opposed to $19,326 for Mexican Americans and $26,770 for Cubans. Among Hispanics, Puerto Ricans bear more of the signs of an under class. From 1956 to 1976 out-of-wedlock births among Puerto Ricans in the United States rose from 11 percent to 46 percent.[4] Among Hispanics, Puerto Ricans have the highest percentage (43.3) of female-headed households with no husband present.[5]

Arriving on the mainland at a time when national parishes were no longer in vogue and without their own priests to minister to them, Puerto Ricans suffered much from bigotry and intolerance. Twenty-five years after the zenith of the migration in the 1950s, they had few vocations. "We have three native Puerto Rican priests in this country," Pablo Sedillo, director of the Secretariat for Hispanics, said in the mid-1970s. "There are very few Puerto Ricans in seminaries studying for the priesthood or the religious life."[6] Because this group was fleeing neither political nor religious persecution, there was much less interest in helping its people settle. Moreover, the political benefit evident in the Cuban resettlement was missing.

There were, however, some optimistic notes. The Archdiocese of New York already had an office for the Hispanic apostolate by the early 1960s. As previously mentioned, the

Cursillo was introduced soon after it came to the United States, and it proved an effective tool for renewal. Many priests and seminarians were sent to Ponce, Puerto Rico, to study Spanish. About four hundred English-speaking priests eventually learned some Spanish and became familiar with the culture.[7]

The Cuban Exodus

The greatest church effort to accommodate immigrants all across the nation, but especially in Florida, began in 1959 after the Cuban revolution. The first to come were 3,000 people connected with the overthrown Batista regime. But by the end of the year about 64,000 people had left Cuba. By the time of the Cuban missile crisis in 1962, another 181,000 immigrants had joined them. Though most were from the middle and upper classes, one-fourth of the exiles came from blue-collar jobs.[8] During this time, because of fears that the government would take away the rights of parents, 14,048 children reached Miami without their parents.[9] For twenty months the Catholic Service Bureau of Miami, headed by Msgr. Bryan O. Walsh, provided foster care, a task later assumed by the federal government.

From the Cuban missile crisis in 1962 to 1965 only 55,916 came. But between 1965 and 1971, under a program of family reunification, 297,318 more Cubans arrived. This was followed by another lull, shattered in 1980, when another 120,000 arrived in the boat lift from the port of Mariel. These groups were welcomed by the US government as refugees. In all, taking into account clandestine immigration between 1960 and 1985, 875,000 left Cuba.

While 10 percent of the inhabitants in pre-Castro Cuba were practicing Catholics, as many as 80 percent of the first 100,000 arriving in 1960–61 fit that description (as opposed to 2 percent of those on the Mariel boat lift).[10] The first refugees were almost exclusively whites; the Mariel group was 65 percent black. Overall, 35.3 percent of the immigrants (exclusive of those on the Mariel boat lift) were blue-collar workers.[11] Among the exiles were 135 priests, 49 of whom went to work in the Archdiocese of Miami.

Many adjustments were by made the church in Miami to minister to the Cubans. Priests were sent to Puerto Rico to study language and culture. By the end of 1962 seven parishes had special Masses with sermons in Spanish. By 1966 there were eight Spanish-speaking priests, with sixteen parishes offering Mass in Spanish. In the first months of the exodus, the church spent $1 million to help the immigrants and, even though the federal Cuban Refugee Emergency Assistance Program (enacted in 1961) was contributing the bulk of the assistance, that amount had grown to $2.5 million by 1965. *The Voice*, the diocesan paper, began a Spanish column in 1959. Later it was expanded to a special section with its own staff,[12] and finally, to a separate paper. By 1988 *La Voz*, the Spanish edition of the diocesan paper, had a circulation of about twenty-five thousand.

As a result of the Cuban influx, two high schools for boys and one for girls were established in 1961. The staff consisted of priests, sisters, and brothers from Cuba. Bilingual programs became an integral part of the curriculum of the Catholic schools; 45 percent of the students were Spanish speaking by 1975. Eleven new parishes were established to serve the refugees. Spanish-speaking associate directors and staff members were appointed to major departments of the chancery. The archdiocesan seminary became bilingual and bicultural, a model for the rest of the nation. By the end of 1980 Hispanics made up 39 percent of the population of metropolitan Miami. Estimates of the number of Catholics ranged from 500,000 to 850,000, with Hispanics accounting for 63 percent and Haitians 7 percent. Two Cuban priests had been ordained bishops by 1988, Agustín Román, auxiliary in Miami, and Enrique San Pedro, a Jesuit who served first as an auxiliary in the Diocese of Galveston-Houston and then as the bishop of the Diocese of Brownsville, Texas, where he died in the 1990s. Román retired in 2003. By then Felipe Estevez, another native Cuban priest, born on the island like Román, had been ordained a bishop.

Father Mario Vizcaino, another priest who came from Cuba, became director of the Southeast Regional Office for Hispanics and also of the Southeast Pastoral Center and continued in those posts in 2005. Msgr. Orlando Fernández, the vicar for Hispanics, was also ordained a bishop. Father Raúl Del Valle, who died in 1988, was the chancellor of the Archdiocese of New York. A Cuban layman, José Debasa, was appointed finance director of the Archdiocese of Los Angeles by then-archbishop Roger Mahony.

A trickle of migration continued into the twenty-first century, but many of those who attempted the crossing were caught by the Coast Guard and returned home.

The Mexican Migrations

The *bracero* program, instituted during World War II to relieve a labor shortage, brought more and more of these seasonal workers in the postwar period. In its peak year, 1956, a total of 445,197 Mexicans labored throughout the nation. Nonetheless, more workers were available than the *bracero* program accepted. Hundreds of thousands crossed the border during that period. By then other industries had seen the value of the cheap labor Mexicans could provide. Many worked in the garment industry, in hotels as maids, in restaurants as busboys and dishwashers, in affluent residential areas as servants and gardeners, and in thousands of sweatshops.

Following the pattern established in the 1920s and 1930s, the Immigration and Naturalization Service (INS) carried out a massive deportation in the early 1950s. From the earliest part of the twentieth century Mexicans had been viewed as "temporary visitors to the United States" who were content to return to Mexico when not needed.[13] Counting those apprehended as they tried to enter the United States illegally, Operation Wetback expelled 3.8 million Mexicans in the course of several years. The INS boasted in its 1955 annual report: "The so-called 'wetback' problem no longer exists. . . . The border has been secured." But by 1973 the INS found it necessary to begin more mass roundups, which continued on a sporadic basis into the 1980s.

In 1964 Congress canceled the *bracero* program by refusing to renew Public Law 78, the authority under which it was carried out. But illegal immigration or migration (some experts insist most Mexicans come only to work temporarily) increased dramatically. The year the *bracero* program was canceled, only 43,844 persons were apprehended at the border for trying to enter without permission. By 1977 such arrests had increased to 954,778.[14] In the 1980s more than a million were turned away each year. The tradition going back to the 1880s of coming to work in the United States could not be nullified simply by canceling the *bracero* program. A study made in the 1970s showed that many of the illegals then had fathers who had been *braceros*.[15]

Meanwhile, conditions in Mexico were forcing more and more workers north. The country had too many people for the arable land available. Unemployment and under-employment in Mexico in 1977 was 30 percent.[16] Not just lack of employment but also lack of well-paid jobs stimulated the migration. At the same time, inflation was rampant. Successive devaluations in the 1970s and 1980s created a bigger gap between earning power in Mexico and in the United States, even at minimum-wage levels. The result was an unprecedented flow of workers across the border.

In the United States this phenomenon was expressed in terms of an invasion by former Marine General Leonard Chapman, who was commissioner of immigration from 1973 to 1977. He toured the country warning that the illegals, whom he estimated to number as many as twelve million, could bring catastrophe to the country. Though other experts declared that many Mexicans came only for six months to a year and that the number of these workers did not exceed four or five million, Chapman's views caused public alarm and rising violence along the border. Polls showed that as high as 82 percent of the American people favored rounding up the illegals and sending them back. The Ku Klux Klan offered to place its own patrols along the border.

A massive effort began in 1994 to stop undocumented immigrants at the Mexican border. Ten thousand new Border Patrol agents were hired. Steel walls and other barriers went up at major crossing points, especially between upper and lower California and at some points in Texas, forcing the undocumented to cross desert and mountain areas. As a result, the number of those who die attempting the crossing has increased to one a day. But the workers continue to come. Some are refugees from oppressive regimes, others victims of hunger and want, caused by many factors, not least the North American Free Trade Agreement enacted in 1994, which has enabled US corporations to drive small shops and industries out of business.

The church was slow to develop a coherent position. It opposed illegal immigration and the *bracero* program in its later stages because it thought that would enable the domestic farm workers to organize. That position, however, was not consistent with church doctrine that there is a prior natural right of persons to immigrate when there is a need.[17] In the ensuing debate over illegal immigration, Catholics more often voiced the view that the nation had a right to sovereignty over its borders.

Despite such ambivalence, the church did speak out on occasion when the rights of immigrants were violated. In 1976 an Arizona rancher and his two sons were accused of kidnapping and torturing three workers who had entered the country illegally. In 1979, due to pressure by a coalition that included Hispanics, the United States Catholic Conference, and individual Catholic clergy, religious women, and laity, the sons were indicted—the father had died in the meantime—and one of them was convicted after a state trial and two federal trials. Among the bishops, Roger Mahony of Stockton, California, and

Patricio Flores of San Antonio stood out for denouncing violence against the illegal workers. Mahony, when he was the ordinary of the Diocese of Stockton, once led a procession of hundreds of persons to the local offices of INS. Throughout the years church personnel frequently served on advisory committees of the US Commission on Civil Rights dealing with immigration problems.

New Refugees

Meanwhile, new refugees from Central America joined the flow. Large communities of Salvadorans, Guatemalans, and Nicaraguans, fleeing war and political repression, established themselves in San Francisco, Los Angeles, New York, and Washington, D.C. In the 1980s, with the Reagan administration's decision to seek military solutions to the problems of Central America, the exodus increased. Over a few years hundreds of thousands of new refugees arrived. Detention centers formerly filled with Mexican illegals were now housing Central Americans. The administration took the position that they didn't qualify under the 1980 Refugee Act, which defined refugees as persons forced to flee because of fear of or the actual experience of persecution. Administration officials claimed that the Central Americans came for economic reasons. Though the church was deeply involved in trying to help the refugees, the bishops took the cautious position of opposing the war and speaking about rights without openly supporting those priests, religious men and women, and laity willing to risk prosecution by providing concrete assistance. Even the Hispanic bishops, who might have chosen a prophetic role, remained largely on the sidelines. The risks were taken by poor Hispanics in the barrios along the Rio Grande, a few priests and nuns throughout the nation, and some Protestant and Jewish clergy, and laity. Barrio residents, parishes, and religious orders provided hospitality when the refugees came to their doors. Some religious orders and societies contributed to pay for the legal services to win political asylum for the refugees.

In El Paso, Annunciation House, a house of hospitality established by layman Rubén García, took in anyone who knocked on the door. In 1980 Mark and Louise Zwick, former lay missioners, founded Casa Juan Diego, a Catholic Worker house in Houston that has provided hospitality to thousands of refugees and other immigrants. The most thankless work on the border, the struggle for human rights, was carried out principally by the American Friends Service Committee's border project, headed since 1983 by Roberto Martínez, a fifth-generation Mexican American. With a small staff, Martínez documented abuses, spoke to victims, monitored high-speed chases that killed dozens and injured hundreds of immigrants, and brought violations to the attention of federal officials. On at least ten occasions over the years he received death threats from individuals or groups, including one from the Ku Klux Klan and another from a local militia. In the 1990s he was wondering how long he could endure. But at the same time, he added, "Every time I ask myself why I am doing this, thinking that I have to get out, one more person comes in injured. I see the pain and suffering and think I am not doing too badly. I just have to deal with the mental anguish. There are so few voices out there to protect the immigrants. If I can do something to make their lives better, I should do it."[18]

Along the border the most courageous bishop was John Fitzpatrick of Brownsville. He supported Casa Oscar Romero, which at one time housed five hundred refugees. Bishop Raymundo Peña of El Paso provided the building García used for Annunciation House. But Bishop Rene Gracida of Corpus Christi, when asked to comment after one of his pastors was arrested and charged with transporting refugees to the interior, was quoted in the press as saying the priest had made an error in judgment.

Eventually, in the 1980s, some religious congregations and parishes declared themselves sanctuaries for the refugees.

Claretian Father Luis Olivares, pastor of Our Lady Queen of Angels in Los Angeles, opened the church every night so that scores of refugees could sleep in the pews. Father Michael Kennedy, a Jesuit, ran the parish's refugee center. Jesuits at Dolores Mission and at several houses sheltered refugees. Parishes in the Diocese of Rockville Centre on Long Island, New York, made similar efforts.

In Tucson and across the Mexican border several Protestant churches and Catholic parishes joined together to provide sanctuary. The leaders of this effort were indicted and tried on various charges. While the Bishops' Committee for Hispanic Affairs was meeting in a retreat house near Tucson, getting an orientation on the pastoral plan voted upon by the Third National Encuentro, the defendants were fighting for their freedom in federal court downtown. None of the bishops visited the courtroom to show solidarity with the defendants.

On November 5, 1986, Congress passed the Immigration Reform and Control Act, a law that had been debated for years. Its aim was to enable the United States to regain control of its borders by stopping the flow of illegals. To do that it became a crime for employers to hire them. At the same time, Congress made those who could prove they had entered the country prior to January 1, 1982, eligible for an amnesty that would eventually lead to citizenship. While the USCC had opposed employer sanctions, the bishops as a group did not oppose the law because they favored the amnesty program. Between May 5, 1987, and May 4, 1988, 1.8 million refugees applied for amnesty. The Migration and Refugee Services Department of the USCC and many dioceses cooperated with the INS in bringing the illegals in to apply for the amnesty. Roger Mahony, by then promoted to archbishop of Los Angeles, cooperated most closely with the INS in the legalization effort. He said the church should assist as many as possible to win amnesty and then seek to change the law to include those who had been left out: refugees and other persons who had entered the country without permission after 1982. The law, however, led to widespread discrimination against citizens or legal immigrants who appeared foreign (Hispanics and Asians). In November 1988 the bishops at their annual meeting in Washington approved a statement expressing their opposition to employer sanctions. But it was unclear whether, having gone along with the law in 1986, their voice would have much effect now.

In the 1990s and 2000s the growing death toll at the Mexican border challenged churches of all denominations. Between the time Operation Gatekeeper had begun in 1994, doubling the size of the Border Patrol and sealing off the easiest crossings with steel walls and sophisticated surveillance technology, and the year 2000, six hundred immigrants had died trying to enter California. Along the entire two-thousand-mile border between the United States and Mexico, seven hundred died in three years, the *Los Angeles Times* reported in the summer of 2000. The same year, according to National Public Radio, thirty-four died attempting to cross in the El Paso area. The toll had risen so alarmingly that, according to news reports, Border Patrolmen were receiving training in first aid and carrying water and high-energy bars to aid those in trouble.

Immigrants provided much of the Hispanic leadership in the church. Ten of the first twenty Hispanic bishops in the United States were immigrants: two from Mexico, two from Cuba, two from Spain, two from Puerto Rico,[19] one from Ecuador, and one from Venezuela. Most of the others were the sons of immigrants. Of 1,954 Hispanic priests in the United States, fewer than two hundred were native born. The proportion of native born among the 1,300 sisters and brothers was similar. Furthermore, at the beginning of the twenty-first century most seminarians were immigrants or the sons of immigrants.

Hispanic immigrants now headed many important offices in the church. For example, Mario Paredes, a Chilean, led the Northeast Regional Office for Hispanics until his retirement in the 2000s; Father Mario Vizcaino, a Cuban, the Southeast Regional Office; Father Ricardo Chavez, son of Mexican immigrants, the West Coast office. Araceli Cantero, a Spaniard, served as the editor of *La Voz*, the highly successful Spanish edition of the diocesan newspaper of the Archdiocese of Miami; Julio Alejandro Escalona, a Mexican, edited the Spanish edition of the *Chicago Catholic*. That pattern held throughout the rest of the nation. Of Hispanic women highlighted in a 2003 Catholic News Service article for assuming leadership posts—for example, as professors, diocesan directors of the Hispanic ministry, and director of the graduate program in Hispanic pastoral ministry at a Jesuit university—most were immigrants.

Traditionally, immigrants have revitalized the church in the United States. Hispanics are no exception.

Chapter 8

Hispanic American Protestantism in the United States

Edwin E. Sylvest, Jr.

A history of the Hispanic church in the United States would be incomplete without a chapter on those who have joined Protestant denominations. Since it is appropriate that that history be written by a Protestant, I asked Dr. Edwin Sylvest, Jr., a faculty member of the Perkins School of Theology at Southern Methodist University, to write this chapter.

Though the overwhelming majority of Hispanics are Catholics, Protestant—mainline as well as evangelical and Pentecostal groups—have always presented a challenge. In the 1980s, a time of greater ecumenical understanding, Catholic bishops were alarmed at the accelerating rate of conversion of Hispanics to Protestant churches, then about sixty thousand a year. Sociologist Father Andrew Greeley, among others, called this an ecclesiastical failure of unprecedented proportions.

The trend continued, if not accelerated, despite church efforts. As of 2000, 9.5 million out of 35 million Hispanics in the United States were Protestants, the vast majority members of Penetecostal churches.

Failure of the Catholic Church to minister adequately to its Hispanic members is seen as an important cause of conversions. Catholics feel that Protestant churches, typically with small congregations, are more hospitable and build a stronger sense of community. Furthermore, they offer ministers who are from the people themselves, that is, Hispanics. The approach of these churches, particularly that of the evangelicals, is considered more affective, perhaps better attuned to Hispanic culture.

Nevertheless, as Sylvest's essay suggests, the experience of Hispanic Protestants has not been as happy as some Catholics imagine. While proportionately more have been able to take part in ordained ministry, they have often occupied the same second-class status that may have led them to leave the Catholic Church.

—MOISES SANDOVAL

A Conquered People: Protestant Response
(1821–1898)

Texas was the place where Protestant Christianity and Hispanic culture made initial contact within the present limits of the United States. Anglo settlers began making their way into Texas and Coahuila, a frontier province of New Spain, in the waning years of the second decade of the nineteenth century. After Mexico became an independent nation in 1821, the government encouraged colonization in Texas and Coahuila. Stephen F. Austin and his colony of San Felipe were among the first Anglos to benefit from Mexican immigration policy.

Although Anglo colonists were required officially to become Roman Catholic, Protestant practice was tolerated. As a result, Protestant missionaries traveled freely, preaching to the burgeoning Anglo population. By 1833 Baptists, Methodists, and Cumberland Presbyterians had established congregations and erected church buildings. Any Protestant ministry to Mexicans was coincidental to serving the religious needs of Anglo colonists, who were culturally Protestant, if not actively participating church people. During this period the normative pattern of Protestant outreach to Mexicans was through distribution of the scriptures. In 1833 Sumner Bacon, a Cumberland Presbyterian minister, was commissioned a colporteur of the American Bible Society, supplying Spanish bibles until his death in 1844. David Ayres, a Methodist layman, undertook a similar ministry during the same period. Both discovered great interest in the Bible among the Spanish-speaking population, notwithstanding the opposition of Roman Catholic priests to its distribution. Some were eager to purchase the book.[1]

With the independence of Texas in 1836 came greater freedom for missionary activity among Spanish speakers. Protestant mission boards and churches, however, continued to be interested primarily in the Anglos. Efforts with Hispanics were regarded as tactics in a larger strategy of missionary activity in Mexico. Robert Blair, the first Protestant missionary officially assigned to work with Spanish-speaking people, viewed his work as an opportunity to learn the language so that he might undertake to enlighten the "semi-heathen, semi-Catholics who use the Spanish language in Mexico."[2]

Blair established a school, Aranama College, to train Mexican youth for missionary work in their native land. The college was short lived but the concept endured well into the present century as a primary means of missionary outreach to Mexico, and eventually to Mexican Americans.

Allowing for good intention and sincere motivation, it is nonetheless evident that the ministry of Protestant churches during this contact period was an instrument of marginalization. A people already victimized by changing political and economic systems suffered the further insult of being of only secondary importance to the religious establishment of Anglo settlers. Lack of comprehensive planning was due not to respect and concern for the development of a more adequate Roman Catholic ministry (that was badly needed) but to the insidious racism and ethnocentrism that unfortunately characterized the Anglo Saxon Protestant ethos of the United States.

The New Southwest (1846–1869)

Though war with Mexico interrupted missionary activity in Texas, the resolution of the conflict through the Treaty of Guadalupe Hidalgo created a much larger field. Mexico lost half of its territory and the population centers in New Mexico and California. Mexicans who chose not to "remove" to the Republic of Mexico became citizens of the United States— Hispanic Americans. But though "regeneration" of native peoples had figured importantly as justification for the war and annexation of territory, Methodists, Baptists, and Presbyterians who began almost immediately to work in New Mexico and California focused their interest primarily on the English-speaking population. Attention to Spanish-speaking peoples was focused on Mexico. Returning soldiers spoke of the "moral destitution" of a land never penetrated by "pure Christianity."

Melinda Rankin, a young New England Presbyterian, saw that defeated Mexicans needed to respond:

> Our country had conquered them and subjugated them to its own terms; and was there nothing more demanded for this bleeding, riven and desolated country? Were there no hearts to commiserate the helpless condition of these perishing millions of souls under the iron heel of papal power, with all its soul-destroying influences? I could not avoid the impression that an important duty devolved upon Evangelical Christendom to try to do something for the moral elevation of this people, who had so long been sitting in the region of the shadow of death.[3]

Rankin established a school for girls in Brownsville, Texas, and distributed bibles. Both efforts duplicated the patterns already established in Texas by Bacon and Ayers, and both efforts were primarily aimed at Mexico, where Rankin went in 1851.

Though only of secondary interest, Mexican Americans began to respond. They were especially interested in the Bible and read it avidly as it became available. In New Mexico, where the Methodist Episcopal Church appointed a missionary in 1853, the Bible brought the first recorded convert to Protestantism. Ambrosio Gonzáles reported: "It was to me a new book. I read until the chickens were crowing for day. I lay down on the lounge in the same room and soon fell asleep. When I woke the sun was shining through the window into my face. The Sun of Righteousness was shining brightly in my soul. I have been a Christian and a Protestant ever since."[4]

Gonzáles became a Methodist class leader in Peralta, where in sixteen years (1855–71) he developed a class of forty-two persons. Lay leadership exemplified by Gonzáles was strengthened as the first Hispanic Americans became members of the clergy. In 1853 Benigno Cardenas, a dissident Roman Catholic priest, became the first ordained Protestant clergyman in the newly acquired territories. He preached his first sermon as a Methodist on the Plaza in Santa Fe on November 20, 1853.

Some Hispanic Americans, eager to assimilate into the life of the new nation, converted to Protestant Christianity. The churches were pleased to count them among their members but failed to entrust them with significant institutional leadership. Anglo missionaries and pastors supervised their work. An internal colony of the United States was being formed, and the churches, Roman Catholic and Protestant, were part of the process.

Missionary Renewal and Institutional Growth (1869–1889)

The Civil War disrupted missionary activity among Hispanics, but a resurgence occurred after the conflict ended. The story of Alejo Hernandez illustrates the complex and conflicting forces in Hispanic American Protestantism during this period.[5] Hernandez, a Catholic seminarian in Mexico when the French set out to establish the Austrian Maximilian as emperor of Mexico, left the seminary in 1862, disgusted with the support the hierarchy gave the imperial experiment. Joining the liberal army of Benito Juarez, Hernandez was captured by the French and eventually crossed the Rio Bravo (the Mexican name for the Rio Grande) in 1869 in search of a Spanish bible.

While in northern Mexico, Hernandez had acquired one of many tracts the American Tract Society asked soldiers of General Zachary Taylor to distribute to the local population during their invasion of Mexico in 1846. It was a piece of nativistic propaganda entitled *Evenings with the Romanists* whose frequent reference to scripture motivated Hernandez to search for a vernacular text of the Bible.

One day while walking in Brownsville, Hernandez was lured by congregational singing into a small Protestant church. Although he could not speak English, he was so moved that he went to the altar at the close of the service and dedicated himself to God. But when he returned to Mexico and attempted a ministry, he experienced such persecution and frustration that he came back to Texas. In Corpus Christi in 1871 he was licensed to preach by the Methodist Episcopal Church, South, ordained a deacon, and appointed to do missionary work among Hispanics in Texas.

But since Methodists were eager to develop their work in Mexico, Alejo Hernandez was appointed to begin a ministry in Mexico City. Failing health caused him to return to Corpus Christi, where he died in 1875. His work opened the possibility of developing Hispanic leadership for Spanish-speaking Protestantism in Texas.

While Anglo leadership continued in the development of Hispanic American Protestantism, an important milestone had been reached. Alexander Sutherland, Thomas Harwood, Henry Pratt, Una Roberts Lawrence, among others, played important roles, but so did José Policarpo Rodríguez, Santiago Tafolla, Trinidad Armendariz, José Marra Botello. Though missionary Protestantism would prevail for another half-century, Hispanic American Protestantism was achieving its own voice, though it was muted.

In the effort to develop Hispanic American clergy, the Protestant churches established a lower standard of preparation. Academic requirements deemed important for Anglo ministers were regarded as unnecessary for Spanish speakers to serve their own people. Their curriculum was essentially a concentrated course in the scriptures. It was felt that to do more would elevate Hispanic ministers beyond their prospective parishioners and create barriers. Furthermore, if pastors were not encouraged to achieve a fully comprehensive education, they would not be lured into secular occupations.[6] The pattern of undertrained and underpaid clergy, dependent on Anglo patronage was established.

Membership increased, clergy developed, and institutional structures were formed and grew, but Hispanic Americans were relegated to secondary status in their own churches. Their Anglo patrons deemed this to be in the interest of the mission.

The essential patterns and structures of Hispanic American Protestantism in the Southwest were fixed in the years from 1869 to 1890. Anglos retained control of the churches and their institutions. Instead of building self-determination, the schools assured assimilation and accommodation to the customs and institutional interests of the conquering culture. Training of indigenous leaders was generally an expedient rather than an affirmation of the values and gifts of the other culture.

New People, New Ministries (1890–1930)

Increased immigration from Mexico beginning in the 1880s and peaking in the 1920s created new challenges for the churches in the Southwest. After the imperialist war with Spain in 1898, the Hispanic populations of Cuba, Puerto Rico, and the Philippines became important areas of missionary endeavor. Indeed, concern for mission among those peoples was part of the ethos that led the United States to occupy those territories. New ties led to significant emigration from the islands, adding to the Cuban and Puerto Rican exiles already living in the United States prior to the war. Cuban enclaves in Tampa, Key West, and Miami experienced Protestant missionary activity. After the Cuban Revolution in 1959 many Cuban pastors came as refugees who served their own as well as other Hispanic communities.

The cultural ethos of these Caribbean immigrants was somewhat different from that of Mexicans and other Hispanics in the Southwest. Among the immigrants were Protestants who had responded to missionary activity in their homelands. Especially in Cuba and Puerto Rico, Protestant missionary activity had been undertaken by exiles who had returned home with their own newfound faith.[7]

For some, Protestantism represented the ideal of liberty and democracy associated with the struggle for independence on the islands and for reform in Mexico. In both instances the Roman Catholic Church was perceived as reactionary and an obstacle to desired transformation. Those attitudes were exploited and reinforced by some Protestant missionaries. As in the case of Alejo Hernandez in Texas, resentment against the hierarchy was reinforced by nativist sentiment in the United States and helped to develop strong anti-Catholic feeling among the immigrants. Such attitudes alienated some Protestant Hispanics from important elements of their own cultural heritage. In a nation that tended to welcome their labor but not them or their cultural traditions, many Hispanic Protestants were further alienated within their own communities.[8]

Response to the needs for service characterized much of the Protestant ministry during the years of the Mexican Revolution and World War I. The mainline Protestant churches developed schools and community centers. Besides adding to the congregational rolls, the immigrant population provided new leaders as well. From among the immigrants came persons with the education facilitating leadership development in the institutional life of the churches.

In southern California, where Hispanics were expanding rapidly, much of the impetus was to "Americanize" the Mexicans. Anglo Protestants worried that abysmal living and working conditions would lead the immigrants to opt for other political alternatives. As Presbyterian and Methodist executives saw it, the "question which is to be decided in the next few years is whether they [the Mexicans] are to be won to anarchy or Americanism; to Bolshevism or to democracy; to Trotsky or Christ."[9]

Not all concern for Americanization was motivated by the presumed socialist threat. Some Protestants felt a genuine, if paternalistic, desire to train men and women helping to develop the country. "Cut out the Mexicans and you cut out a large factor in our industries. Educate them and you add a sound and useful aid to our country's development, especially here in the Southwest."[10] Mexicans had, after all, built railroads, worked in the development of mines and the steel industry, and were engaged in producing food.

Despite such concern for the well-being of Mexican Americans, the churches did not resist the mistreatment of those repatriated during the Great Depression. Many Mexicans, welcomed when their services were needed, were sent "back where they came from." Many native-born Americans, especially those without documents, were deported too. Pastoral care and social services did not address the systemic marginalization of Hispanics in the United States.

Institutional Success and Popular Challenge (1930–2005)

This period saw the development of a new concept of community-based Christian ministry that addressed the needs of the whole person. "Houses of Neighborliness" and community centers became so important in some communities that the people began to regard them as "theirs" and to "secularize" them. Neighborhood priorities displaced the evangelistic emphases and strained relationships with the churches that conceived the centers as places where evangelization, if not proselytism, might occur.

Sponsoring denominational agencies, often related to churches committed to the growing movement of Protestant ecumenism, found it difficult to employ the neighborhood facilities in their evangelistic strategies because ecumenical ministries involved Roman Catholics in forming policy for the centers. Many centers were allowed to become relatively independent secular agencies.

Anglo sponsors as well as many "pietistic" Hispanic congregations, offended by the social activism of the centers, resisted the success of these ministries. That resistance became increasingly evident during the 1960s when Hispanics displayed great ambivalence toward many of the activities of *La Raza*.

The tensions in the community-center ministries signaled an awareness that systemic issues would need to be addressed if the hopes of Hispanic immigrants were to be realized and if justice for the entire Hispanic American community was to be achieved. Service-oriented ministries met needs that certainly required attention, but they did not create communities of reciprocity. Indeed, when reciprocity was achieved, enabling Hispanic Americans to participate in making policy, the service ministries became problematic for their sponsors.

The Hispanic American community itself saw the challenge to traditional structures as a threat. For some, the issue was that of the church's proper relationship to the world and a concept of salvation that envisioned human fulfillment and final justice as eschatological hopes. For others, a challenge to the system compromised long-held dreams and hard-won institutional successes. By the mid-1930s some Hispanic Americans had received formal theological education, had been ordained like their Anglo counterparts, and had been appointed to positions of major responsibility within their denominational structures. There was reason to hope that shared power and responsibility would replace dependence and patronage.

In the Methodist Church, for example, Hispanics carried leadership responsibility and authority in conference structures. In the Texas Mexican Conference, predecessor of the Rio Grande Annual Conference, Alfredo Nañez, the first Hispanic American Methodist to complete his formal theological education with the B.D. degree from Southern Methodist University, and Francisco Ramos were named Presiding Elders. In similar fashion a Latin American Provisional Conference was established in southern California in 1941. Although in both cases Hispanic leaders worked under Anglo bishops and mission executives, they enjoyed significant autonomy in decision-making and administration.[11]

Many Hispanic Americans who served in the military during World War II began to envision full and equal participation in US institutions, including the churches. Many felt that complete assimilation into the mainstream would bring greater benefit from the economic and political systems, a dream also shared by Anglos. The decision of the US Supreme Court in *Brown vs. The Board of Education* developed widespread impetus to eliminate segregation, which existed in the churches as well as in the civil society. Presbyterians in Texas ended the Texas Mexican Presbytery and merged its congregations into other presbyteries. The Methodist Latin American Provisional Conference in California was also integrated into other structures.

Uncritical Anglo idealism, Hispanic desire for full participation, and economic opportunity all contributed to decisions to integrate. Unfortunately, the Hispanic Americans and others were expected to adopt the culture of the Anglo majority. Hispanic Americans and Anglos were to be equal participants, but in an Anglo system. Some Presbyterians in Texas refused to integrate on that basis and attempted to form an independent Spanish-speaking Protestant church. They failed for lack of resources and adequate leadership.[12]

Many Hispanic Methodists in California viewed the decision to integrate their conference as a defeat, but the Anglos prevailed. While some ministers were pleased with the economic advantage they gained through improved salaries, the laity saw no advantage in the new arrangement but instead experienced isolation and rejection. Hispanic membership began to decline. By the late 1980s the principle of autonomy and the need to affirm cultural and linguistic values had been reinstituted with the establishment of a Latin American Mission District within the California-Pacific Annual Conference. The first Hispanic American bishop in the United Methodist Church, Elias Galvan, was elected in 1984 by the Western Jurisdiction, which includes California.

In Texas and New Mexico the Rio Grande Conference, which was established in 1939 when Methodist Episcopal churches of the South and the North merged with the Methodist Protestant Church to become the Methodist Church, resisted pressures to merge with Anglo conferences. Although it needs economic help from the denomination, the Rio Grande Conference has developed strong Hispanic leadership that contributes to the national church and to the development of ministries within the region. Two of the presiding Hispanic American bishops of the United Methodist Church were formed through the ministry of the Rio Grande Conference. Joel Martínez was the first Hispanic American bishop to preside over the conference, and Minerva Carcaño, a significant leader in the Rio Grande Conference, was elected by the Western Jurisdiction to serve there.

The use of Spanish and an appreciation of the cultural heritage are important elements of the self-understanding of the Rio Grande Conference, but because many of the younger members no longer speak Spanish, ministers in full connection must be bilingual and practice bilingual worship in many congregations. That very bilingualism, so important to the new *mestizaje* of Hispanic Americans in a historically predominant Anglo society, may be the reason why mainline churches, with the exception of the Southern Baptists, show little or no growth in total membership at a time when Hispanics are the fastest growing group in the country. Much of that growth occurs in the most marginal sectors of the Hispanic community, sectors where bilingualism may be a requirement of the work place but not in the household or the neighborhood,

Language affinity and the burgeoning immigrant population, predominantly from Mexico, but actually from all of Latin

America, where Pentecostal/Charismatic Christianity has been growing so dramatically, may be factors in the surging growth of Pentecostalism among Hispanic Americans in the United States. More than three-fourths of the approximately 9.5 million Hispanic American Protestants are Pentecostal.

As the Hispanic population in the nation grows and Anglo conferences and churches begin to respond with outreach ministries, the Rio Grande Conference and other mainline Hispanic Protestant groups find potential new resources for developing outreach and, at the same time, come under criticism because their concepts of ministry do not always mirror the perceptions of Anglo decision-makers. The growing awareness of the need for Hispanic ministry brings with it controversy and threat. The United Methodist General Conference of 1988, responding to the petition of MARCHA, the Hispanic caucus, created a quadrennial study commission to develop a comprehensive plan for Hispanic ministry throughout the whole church. Presbyterians, Lutherans, and others made similar efforts.

One of the earliest and most comprehensive efforts to respond to Hispanics in the United States was undertaken by the United Presbyterian Church in response to the leadership of Jorge Lara-Braud in the 1960s. Ironically, that action by the General Assembly came as Hispanics were becoming a less significant element than they had been a decade earlier.

Southern Baptist mission agencies have been particularly effective in developing Hispanic ministries. Among traditional Protestant churches the Southern Baptists have the largest Hispanic membership. They permit a degree of local autonomy that facilitates flexibility in responding to the needs and interests of particular congregations, though Hispanic churches appear to be well assimilated into denominational structures, problematic as they are for all Southern Baptists.

Efforts by mainline Hispanic Protestants to sustain strong denominational affiliations have affected pastoral responses to issues of social justice. In some cases Anglo congregations have responded more directly than the Hispanics.

There was no evident response, however, by either Anglo or Hispanic Protestants during the Zoot Suit riots of the 1940s. While the city of Los Angeles watched passively and Methodist Hispanics were preoccupied with making the Latin American Provisional Conference an effective instrument of ministry, Mexican American young people struggling to discover and express their identity were brutalized by United States naval personnel on leave and by the police. Although the struggle of the Methodists and young people was the same, that is, to assert a cultural and personal identity different than that of the Anglo majority, neither group saw the other as an ally. Indeed, the young people were viewed by Hispanic Protestants as social outcasts. The distance was great between organized Protestantism and "the first people to call themselves Chicanos."[13]

Protestantism and Social Protest

As the Chicano movement developed during the 1960s, the distance between it and the churches narrowed in some respects, though it continued to be problematic. Hispanic American Reies Lopez Tijerina, a Pentecostal minister, led the struggle to recover lost land grants in northern New Mexico; Rodolfo "Corky" Gonzáles, a member of the Presbyterian Church, led the urban struggle in Denver. The Migrant Ministry of the National Council of Churches was an early supporter of Cesar Chavez and his farm workers.

There was, however, little or no participation of the churches as institutions. Though individual Hispanic Protestants, lay and clergy, took part in the struggle, few Hispanic congregations ventured forward. Most Hispanic church people reacted as the Anglos did. They were thoroughly integrated into an economic system governed by the interests of agribusiness.[14] As the struggle moved to Texas, some Rio Grande pastors did take great risk to support the farm workers. Joel Martínez, now a bishop, led a march from the Rio

Grande Valley to San Antonio, and the conference eventually adopted a resolution supporting the UFW boycott, but there was great ambivalence among local churches and little enthusiasm for serious and sustained engagement in the struggle.

Individual congregations on the frontier and in the cities responded significantly to the crisis occasioned by the passage of the Immigration Reform and Control Act of 1986. Many Hispanic congregations helped Central American refugees, though none took formal action declaring themselves part of the Sanctuary movement. Response to concrete human need is easier than grappling with the politics of transformation on the larger issues of immigration and foreign policy, although Hispanic caucuses and leaders have helped formulate responses, and there is a growing trend in that direction.

Pentecostalism

Evangelical Christianity has become the most rapidly growing and vigorous movement within Protestantism. (There is also a significant charismatic movement within the Roman Catholic Church.) In the Hispanic American population evangelicalism, especially Pentecostalism, has grown rapidly, as in Latin America, and in its various forms has become the predominant expression of Hispanic Protestantism. Pentecostalism has become mainline among Hispanic American Protestants.

A growing social consciousness and the implications of Christian faith for social justice and public policy are now clearly evident in both mainline Protestantism and Pentecostalism. Though the two movements are frequently in conflict and seem mutually exclusive to many Hispanic Protestants, they do arise from common roots in the life experience of the people and in the Christian gospel itself. Should the two movements converge in congregational life and denominational institutions, Hispanic Protestantism may emerge as an increasingly significant influence within US society.

There are signs of such convergence at denominational and regional levels. Indeed, signs of mutual respect and cooperation are developing among Pentecostal, other evangelical, mainline Protestant, and Roman Catholic churches. A limiting circumstance in this evolution is the generally congregational polity of Pentecostal churches. That limitation is offset through the creation of regional structures in places like the Los Angeles and New York metropolitan areas.

Lalive d'Epinay, in his now classic study in Chile, shows that Pentecostalism is at once in radical continuity and disjunction with its historical and social contexts. It understands the essence of popular religious practice and gives it new expression while discarding its traditional forms. It rejects the cult of the saints but affirms the healing power of the spirit; it rejects festival and sacred processions yet is very public in its display of religious enthusiasm; it rejects the camaraderie of the cantina and substitutes the fellowship of nightly worship with stirring music, shared testimony, and prayer. Though against institutional systems of authority, clerical, papal, denominational, it asserts the ancient and no less powerful authority of the cacique. While anyone, by the gift of the Spirit, may emerge as a leader, the selection is not democratic but charismatic. In short, Pentecostal Protestantism represents a fundamental accommodation of the teaching and practice of received traditions and counterposes imposed institutional authority with an authority that grows out of the community itself.[15]

Pentecostalism expresses the real-life experience and struggle of its adherents in forms that are commensurate with their daily experience. Those forms give free expression of the struggle for existence and self-affirmation in environments from which mainline institutions are often removed. The community's life is governed by its struggle to solve the problem of survival in an alien environment and is not concerned with the application of programs created elsewhere and mediated through external structures of authority.[16]

Mainline Protestantism may be easily perceived in many sectors of the Hispanic American community as systems of teaching and institutional interests that do not correspond to the life experience of the community. Those who experience the larger social context as threatening and oppressive may choose a faith expression that recognizes and affirms that experience. Historically, Pentecostal societies tend not to struggle for systemic transformation through political involvement; rather, they create an alternative environment that brings a degree of peace and satisfaction to their adherents and sustains them in their struggle with a hostile world. That form of religion may be perceived as an opiate, or it may be acknowledged as a powerful mode of protest to systemic oppression.

Groups like Esperanza USA, the Alianza de Ministerios Evangélicos Nacionales, the Latino Pastoral Action Center, the National Hispanic Christian Leadership Conference, among others, provide national and regional structures and events that encourage cooperative response to fundamental societal concerns like immigration reform. While such groups open dialogue and encourage social action, the Asociación para la Educación Teológica and the Hispanic Association for Bilingual Bicultural Ministries bridge denominational and ideological divides to foster a growing cadre of Hispanic American Protestants who are prepared to offer sustaining leadership for an emerging Hispanic American ecumenical movement that embraces the strengths of the mainline traditions as it draws energy from the dynamism of Pentecostalism.

A Distinctive Role
for Hispanic American Protestantism

Despite the perpetuation of structures and patterns of dependence for Hispanic Protestants and despite their relatively insignificant numbers, they are integral members of the larger community of *La Raza*. Their Protestant affiliation need not be viewed primarily as a means of acculturation or of escape. Hispanic American Protestants now begin to convert the institutions of their oppressors into instruments of service with the oppressed. Institutionally, such a transformation may never be complete, but Hispanic American Protestants are uniquely situated to put the power and resources of the conqueror's institutions to the service of the conquered. That service will be defined increasingly by Hispanic Americans who choose their Hispanic American Protestant identity as Hispanics and Christians, even as Protestant Christians.[17]

Hispanic Pentecostalism, problematic in many ways, is itself a fundamental challenge to its environing social contexts, civil and ecclesiastic. Something basic to the assertion of human worth and dignity is expressed in the movement. It cannot simply be dismissed as irrelevant and escapist in relation to the struggle for justice. In it the voice of a people finds expression. It is a voice that must not be ignored. Increasingly there are signs that a Hispanic church of the people is stirring within Protestantism and Roman Catholicism. Though relations between these two great Christian traditions are no less problematic now than in the past, in the complex variety of forms and practice there is in continual formation a Hispanic Christian community that is catholic in its concern and ministry and committed to the embodiment in the flesh of *La Raza* of the suffering love of One who died servant of all yet Lord of all, the sign of the coming liberation of all humanity.

Chapter 9

The Future Hispanic Church

Between 2000 and 2004 the number of US Hispanics increased from 35 million to 41.3 million, an 18 percent jump. Their numbers will continue to grow at least until 2050, when the Census Bureau projects a count of 102.6 million.[1] At that time, the bishops' Secretariat for Hispanic Affairs estimates, 85 percent of US Catholics will be Hispanic. In a few years, if not already, the paradigm of a Hispanic church as part of a larger one will no longer apply. If the church then can be divided into parts, the largest one will be Hispanic, at least in race and ethnicity. As Mexican American theologian Virgil Elizondo predicted, the future is mestizo, a diverse mix of nationalities and races, for Hispanics, as the Census Bureau ruled, can be of any race.

Indeed, Hispanics are already the majority in many areas. In Los Angeles, the diocese with the largest population, Hispanics are 65 percent of the parishioners; in some dioceses in Texas and California they are an even larger proportion. They dominate in San Antonio, El Paso, and other Rio Grande Valley dioceses, and in Houston, Miami, and other large cities. Some dioceses, notably Santa Fe and Brownsville, Texas, have always been heavily Hispanic. In the Archdiocese of New York, Hispanics are the largest group by far in the city itself and are not an absolute majority only because upstate counties tip the balance the other way.

Hispanics, however, are not a monolithic group. The category includes Mexicans, Puerto Ricans, Cubans, Spaniards and people from all nations in the Americas, twenty in all. Both recently and long ago some have intermarried with Anglos, Asians, blacks, Middle Easterners, and others. Some have assimilated into mainstream middle-class society and may not even identify themselves as Hispanic, or Latino, as preferred in some regions of the country. Their goals, aspirations, and gifts may differ. Moreover, national loyalties, political ideology, and economic and social class may divide them.

Also, the longer Hispanics live in the United States, the closer they get to the mainstream in views and attitudes, yet not blurring or erasing their cultural identity.[2] All Hispanics, even those with the longest tenure, share language, views, and values different from those of other minorities and non-Hispanic whites.[3] Those values tend to survive even in interracial and interethnic marriages. Thus Hispanics are unlikely to lose their identity in the foreseeable future. "Waves and still more waves have passed over the Spanish-speaking people, but they are still as firmly rooted in the Southwest as a forest of Joshua trees," wrote D. H. Lawrence. "They are not interlopers or immigrants but an indigenous people."[4] There are now Hispanic communities in every part of the country, even in states like Georgia, Arkansas, and Alaska, not the traditional destinations of immigrants. Theirs is a living culture, continually reinforced by new waves of immigrants and refugees from Latin America and also being recovered by those who have been here for generations.

A Hispanic majority, though problematic, is an important stage in the history of the church as a whole. But at least in the first decades of the twenty-first century, Hispanics will be the majority only in the pews. In 2004 only 5 percent of the bishops, priests, nuns, ordained lay deacons, and other ecclesial ministers were Hispanic. Clearly, with the current criteria, the church cannot look to them to solve its vocations crisis. Vocations increased only slightly during the past twenty-five years, with scant hope of dramatic change. Furthermore, the deeper Hispanics move into mainstream society, the less likely they are to choose a religious vocation. That means that, for a long time, their role in church decision-making will be minor. As Hispanic bishops are wont to point out, Hispanics will not be at the table where decisions are made—by bishops, priests, nuns, and the governing councils of religious orders and congregations.

Yet, recent history has shown that individual bishops, priests, nuns, and lay persons can move the institution: the now-retired Archbishop Patricio Flores in his prime; the late Cesar Chavez; Paul Sedillo, former head of the Secretariat for Hispanic Affairs; community organizer Ernesto Cortés, Jr.; and many others. So can clerical, lay, and religious groups, among them PADRES in the 1970s and 1980s, Las Hermanas, the Academy of Catholic Hispanic Theologians in the United States, and the National Catholic Council for Hispanic Ministry.

Then, of course, there is the weight of the population. At least for the first half of the twenty-first century the Catholic Church will continue to grow only because of the fertility, youth, and high immigration of Hispanics and, to a lesser extent, of immigrants from Asia and Africa. Recent statistics show the strength of this immigration. In Los Angeles, eight in ten Hispanics were native born in 1970; in 1995, two-thirds were foreign born.[5] By 2040, Hispanics will become the majority in California, the state where they are most numerous. Of the twenty-one million the state expects to gain by 2050, eighteen million will be Hispanic. In a few decades they will also be the overwhelming majority in Texas, the state with the second largest Hispanic population. Nationally, the white non-Hispanic population, now growing only at a replacement rate, will go into decline, part of a worldwide trend demographers call "one of the most momentous trends in world history."[6] Europe will lose 100 million people in the next fifty years. Fertility is declining in the Third World too, but more slowly. Hispanics will contribute youth, growth, and vitality in a time of population decline.

However, many dioceses continue to operate as if no major changes in demographics were under way. In *Catholic New York*, the monthly of the Archdiocese of New York, the reader sees the model of a melting-pot church, one in which the Irish dominate. Only two pages are in Spanish, often translations of articles aimed at another audience, and none of the bylined writers or columnists is Hispanic. The overall impression is that Hispanics are an insignificant minority. Los Angeles and Miami, on the other hand, with separate diocesan newspapers in Spanish and English, model parallel churches, one for the English-speaking culture and one for the Spanish-speaking. This is the typical model where Hispanics are the majority—parallel institutions, ministries, programs, and organizations, for example, youth ministry for Anglos and youth ministry for Hispanics, *Cursillo* in English and *Cursillo* in Spanish, Mass in English and Mass in Spanish. This model owes more to social distance between Hispanics and mainstream Catholics than to differences in language. In all cases the church for the English speaking, whether or not it is the majority, gets the lion's share of the funds. It is always clear that this group is considered to be more important. The "many faces in God's house" model proposed by Encuentro 2000, in which all the diverse groups are equal, is visible only in large cities where the Mass is celebrated in as many as forty languages. But the tacit assumption is that these accommodations are temporary, that the mainstream culture will remain dominant.

In the past, citing low Mass attendance, inferior knowledge of Catholic doctrine, and the failure to generate vocations, many have argued that Hispanics are not authentic Catholics. Hispanic claims of being the majority in any region or diocese have been contested, as in 1978 when it came to naming a bishop in the then-new Diocese of San Bernardino (California) or a vicar for Hispanics in Denver during the same period. In 1972, when the First National Encuentro was held, Hispanics were considered a problem to be solved, according to one of the speakers at that conference, that is, when their presence was acknowledged at all. More often, their presence was denied. Father Mario Vizcaino, director of the Southeast Regional Office for Hispanics, said some bishops in that region were not convinced they had Hispanics until they were shown the census tracts. When parish histories were written, Hispanics were ignored, even in dioceses in Texas where Anglos have long been a minority. In one of these, a parish in Castroville, some fifty miles from San Antonio, where Hispanics were 80 percent of parishioners, the book dealt only with Anglo families and their contributions. Hispanics were present only in the photos of parish organizations.

Nevertheless, by any measure Hispanics are or will be the majority of Catholics in the nation and the other building blocks of a Hispanic church—culture, organization, ministry, and mission—are going into place. Spanish, the principal vehicle of culture, is clearly the nation's second language, heard on airplanes, radio, and television and in the streets, work places, and churches. Spanish appears on marquees and billboards, notices in public buildings, and hospitals. Bank ATM machines give the customer the option to use English or Spanish. Business promotion mail often comes in both languages. Hispanics are also recovering and practicing their religious and cultural traditions; writing their own history, novels, and poetry; and creating their own theology and liturgical music.

Over the past thirty-five years the diverse Hispanic groups—Mexican Americans, Puerto Ricans, Cubans, Central and South Americans—have learned to work together. With the financial support of the bishops, they planned, organized, and carried out national *encuentros* in 1972, 1977, 1985, and 2000. They established the Mexican American Cultural Center, the Southeast Pastoral Institute, and similar centers in the Northeast, Midwest, and West Coast, as well as regional and diocesan offices for Hispanic ministry and organizations of theologians, liturgists, priests, sisters, and deacons. They organized parishes and other churches in the barrios of San Antonio, Los Angeles, Houston, and El Paso to work for change, thus proving wrong the claim that Hispanics, especially the poor, could not organize.

The late Maryknoll Father Donald Hessler, a missioner in Mexico for nearly half a century, often said that Hispanics would renew the church of the United States. Though the idea was greeted with skepticism, the renewal Hessler predicted has been going on for decades. The *Cursillo* and Marriage Encounter, movements imported from Spain, revitalized the faith of millions of Catholics in the latter half of the twentieth century. Since 1968 the Latin American churches have contributed new theologies, basic Christian communities, and the conclusions of three historic meetings of Latin American bishops in 1968, 1979 and 1989, among them the preferential option for the poor. Here at home the voluntary poverty modeled by Cesar Chavez, founder of the United Farm Workers, raised a new standard of leadership. Also, in a culture excessively materialistic, Hispanic immigrants, working here for the lowest wages, somehow manage to send billions of dollars to their communities back home—a powerful example of living simply and working for the families and communities that sent them. Finally, Latin America contributes the witness of its martyrs, their deaths caused by regimes supported by US foreign policy and, ultimately, the indifference of the American public. The Hispanic church of the future will have strong bonds with the churches in Latin America.

As regards mission, Hispanics model a church more attuned to and respectful of diversity, less materialistic and individualistic, more family and community based, in which faith is mediated by their culture rather than by the dominant secular culture and ideology of the United States. Mexican novelist Carlos Fuentes, writing about Hispanics in the United States, says the universal question of the twenty-first century is how we deal with the "other" at a time of global interdependence and communications. He suggests that the people best prepared to deal with that central issue are Hispanics, who are "Iberian and Greek, Roman and Jewish, Arab, Gothic and Gypsy. Spain and the New World are centers where multiple cultures meet. . . . When we exclude we betray ourselves. When we include, we find ourselves."[7]

Notes

1. The Indigenous Heritage

1. Pablo Richard, "Hermenéutica Bíblica India: Revelación de Dios en las religiones indígenas y en la Biblia (Después de 500 años de dominación)," in *Sentido Histórico del V Centenario (1492–1992)*, ed. Guillermo Meléndez (San José, Costa Rica: DEI, 1992), 55.

2. Carlos Fuentes, *The Buried Mirror: Reflections on Spain and the New World* (New York: Houghton Mifflin, 1992), 346.

3. Daniel Gerard Groody, CSC, *Corazón y Conversión: The Dynamics of Mexican Immigration, Christian Spirituality and Human Transformation* (Ph.D. thesis, Jesuit School of Theology, Berkeley, California, 2000), chap. 4.

4. Juan Schobinger, "Las Religiones Amerindias," in *Resistencia y Esperanza, Historia del Pueblo Cristiano en América Latina y El Caribe*, ed. Guillermo Meléndez (San José, Costa Rica: DEI, 1992), 49.

5. Mario A. Rodríguez León, "Invasion and Evangelization in the Sixteenth Century," in *The Church in Latin America 1492–1992*, ed. Enrique Dussel (Maryknoll, NY: Orbis Books, 1992), 44.

6. Ibid.

7. Richard, "Hermenéutica Bíblica India," 59.

8. Osvaldo Silva, *Prehistoria de América*, 5th ed. (Santiago de Chile: Editorial Univeritaria, 1971).

9. Torre Littmarck, *Gamla Uppsala: From Ancient to Modern Time* (Uppsala, Sweden: Dahlins tryckeri AB, 2002), 34.

2. Conquest, Settlement, and Evangelization

1. Jared Diamond, *Guns, Germs, and Steel: The Fates of Human Societies* (New York: W. W. Norton, 1999), 211.

2. Ibid., 212.

3. Ibid., 360.

4. María de Jesús Ybarra, "Los Hispanos en el Noroeste: Primera Migración, 1774–1820," an unpublished paper citing research by Erasmo Gamboa and T. Hilaire, SJ.

5. Enrique Dussel, "1492: Análisis Ideológico de Las Diferentes Posiciones," in *Sentido Histórico del V Centenario (1492–1992)*, ed. Guillermo Meléndez (San José, Costa Rica: DEI, 1992), 21; see also Enrique Dussel, ed. *The Church in Latin America 1492–1992* (Maryknoll, NY: Orbis Books, 1992), 4.

6. Gustavo Gutiérrez, cited in Mario A. Rodríguez León, "Invasion and Evangelization in the Sixteenth Century," in Dussel, *Church in Latin America 1492–1992*, 43.

7. Edward P. Dozier, *The Pueblo Indians of North America* (New York: Holt, Rinehart and Winston, 1970), 45.

8. Frederick Webb Hodge, George P. Hammond, and Agapito Rey, eds., *Fray Alonso de Benavides' Revised Memorial of 1634* (Albuquerque: The University of New Mexico Press, 1945), 68.

9. Ibid., 80.

10. Dozier, *The Pueblo Indians of North America*, 76.

11. *Encyclopedia Americana* (New York: Americana Corp., 1976), 2:424.

12. Jay P. Dolan, *The American Catholic Experience: A History from Colonial Times to the Present* (New York: Doubleday, 1985), 26.

13. William H. Harris and Judith H. Levy, *The New Columbia Encyclopedia* (New York: Columbia Univ. Press, 1975), 1413.

14. Fray Angelico Chavez, *The Old Faith and Old Glory: The Story of the Church in New México since the American Occupation (1846–1946)* (Santa Fe: Santa Fe Press, 1946), 3.

15. Ibid., 55–56.

16. David J. Weber, *The Mexican Frontier, 1821–1846: The American Southwest under Mexico* (Albuquerque: Univ. of New Mexico Press, 1982), 57.

17. Ibid., 71.

18. Jerome J. Martínez y Alire, "The Influence of the Roman Catholic Church in New Mexico under Mexican Administration: 1821–1848," paper presented at the CEHILA symposium in Las Cruces, New Mexico (January 15–17, 1988).

19. Ibid.

20. Weber, *The Mexican Frontier*, 74.

21. Juan Romero and Moises Sandoval, *Reluctant Dawn: Historia del Padre A. J. Martínez, Cura de Taos* (San Antonio: Mexican American Cultural Center, 1976), 11.

22. Ibid., 14.

23. Albert J. Nevins, MM, *American Martyrs from 1542* (Huntington, IN: Our Sunday Visitor, 1987), 174–76.

24. Angelico Chavez, *My Penitente Land: Reflections on Spanish New Mexico* (Albuquerque: Univ. of New Mexico Press, 1974), 111.

25. Martínez y Alire, "The Influence of the Roman Catholic Church in New Mexico under Mexican Administration."

26. Marta Weigle, *The Penitentes of the Southwest* (Santa Fe: Ancient City Press, 1970), 18.

3. A New Conquest (1848–1890)

1. Jerome Martínez y Alire, "The Influence of the Roman Catholic Church in New Mexico under Mexican Administration," paper presented at the CEHILA symposium in Las Cruces, New Mexico (January 15–17, 1988), 16.

2. Kevin Starr, quoted in Robert Coles, "California, Here I Come," *The New Yorker* (August 6, 1973).

3. Rodolfo Acuña, *Occupied America: A History of Chicanos*, 2nd ed. (New York: Harper and Row, 1981), 17.

4. Edwin Sylvest, Jr., "Hispanic American Protestantism in the United States," in *Fronteras: A History of the Latin American Church in the USA since 1513*, ed. Moises Sandoval (San Antonio: The Mexican American Cultural Center, 1983), 285.

5. Robert F. Heizer and Alan F. Almquist, *The Other Californians* (Berkeley and Los Angeles: Univ. of California Press, 1971), 200.

6. Wayne Moquin with Charles van Doren, eds., *A Documentary History of the Mexican Americans* (New York: Praeger Publishers, 1971), 181.

7. Carey McWilliams, *North from Mexico: The Spanish-Speaking People of the United States* (New York: Greenwood Press, 1968), 110.

8. James A. Michener, *Centennial* (New York: Random House, 1974), 926.

9. McWilliams, *North from Mexico*, 90.

10. Leonard Pitt, *Decline of the Californios* (Berkeley and Los Angeles: Univ. of California Press, 1966), 117.

11. Tiburcio Vasquez, quoted in David F. Gómez, *Somos Chicanos, Strangers in Our Own Land* (Boston: Beacon Press, 1973).

12. Ellwyn R. Stoddard, *Mexican Americans* (Washington, DC: Univ. Press of America, 1973), 5.

13. Juan Seguin, quoted in David J. Weber, *Foreigners in Their Native Land: Historical Roots of the Mexican Americans* (Albuquerque: Univ. of New Mexico Press, 1973), 181.

14. Moises Sandoval and Salvador E. Alvarez, "The Church in California," in Sandoval, *Fronteras*, 220.

15. Ibid.

16. Fray Angelico Chavez, *The Old Faith and Old Glory: 1846–1946* (Santa Fe: Santa Fe Press, 1946), 8.

17. In Lucien Hendren, "The Church in New Mexico," in Sandoval, *Fronteras*, 201.

18. Carmen Tafolla, "Expansion of the Church in Texas," in Sandoval, *Fronteras*, 188.

19. Ibid., 189.

20. Ibid., 188.

21. Jean A. Meyer, *The Cristero Rebellion: The Mexican People between Church and State, 1926–1929* (New York: Cambridge Univ. Press, 1976), 6.

22. Tafolla, "Expansion of the Church in Texas," 188.

23. Francis J. Weber, *Catholic Footprints in California* (Newhall, CA: Hogarth Press, 1970), 219–20.

24. Ibid., 216.

25. Ibid., 212.

26. Michael Neri, cited in Alvarez and Sandoval, "The Church in California," 215.

27. Marta Weigle, *The Penitentes of the Southwest* (Santa Fe: Ancient City Press), 14.

28. Frances Leon Swadesh, *Los Primeros Pobladores* (Notre Dame, IN: Univ. of Notre Dame Press, 1974), 73.

29. Ibid.

30. Ibid., 77.

31. Santiago Valdez, "Biograffía del Presbitero Antonio José Martínez," MS, Huntington Library, 1877, 1:96, cited in Juan Romero and Moises Sandoval, *Reluctant Dawn: Historia del Padre A. J. Martínez, Cura de Taos* (San Antonio: Mexican American Cultural Center, 1976), 15.

32. Ibid., 1.

33. Hendren, "The Church in New Mexico," 203.

34. US Commission on Civil Rights, *Puerto Ricans in the United States: An Uncertain Future* (Washington, DC: US Commission on Civil Rights, October 1976), 11.

4. Growth and Conflict (1890–1946)

1. Jay P. Dolan, *The American Catholic Parish: A History from 1850 to the Present*, 2 vols. (New York: Paulist Press, 1987), 2:81.

2. Carmen Tafoya, "Expansion of the Church in Texas," in *Fronteras: A History of the Latin American Church in the USA since 1513*, ed. Moises Sandoval (San Antonio: Mexican American Cultural Center, 1983), 227.

3. Ibid., 235.

4. Ibid., 236.

5. Dolan, *The American Catholic Parish*, 2:88.

6. Manuel Gamio, *Mexican American Immigration to the United States: A Study of Human Migration and Adjustment* (New York: Dover Publications, 1971), 118.

7. Salvador Alvarez, "The Roots of Mestizo Catholicism in California," in Sandoval, *Fronteras*, 243.

8. Dolan, *The American Catholic Parish*, 83.

9. Alvarez, "The Roots of Mestizo Catholicism in California," 242.

10. Thomas E. Sheridan, *Los Tucsoneneses, The Mexican Community in Tucson, 1854–1941* (Tucson: Univ. of Arizona Press, 1986), 155.

11. Fray Angelico Chavez, *The Old Faith and Old Glory: The Story of the Church in New Mexico since the American Occupation (1846–1946)* (Santa Fe: Santa Fe Press, 1946), 22.

12. Ibid.

13. In Juan Romero and Moises Sandoval, *Reluctant Dawn: Historia del Padre A. J. Martínez, Cura de Taos* (San Antonio: Mexican American Cultural Center, 1976), 14, citing talk on vocations by Chavez at PADRES retreat in February 1970, in which he quoted Gerken on why he recruited Mexican Americans for the seminary he founded in Albuquerque.

14. Chavez, *The Old Faith and Old Glory*, 30.

15. Dolan, *The American Catholic Parish*, 2:85.

16. *Progress Report*, Bishops' Committee for the Spanish Speaking (May 1 to November 1, 1946).

17. Raymond McGowan, "History and Necessity of the Catholic Council for the Spanish Speaking," in Catholic Councils for the Spanish Speaking, *Proceedings of the Tenth Annual Conference* (April 1960), 30

18. *History of the Immigration and Naturalization Service*, a report prepared by the Senate Judiciary Committee for the Select Commission on Immigration and Refugee Policy, Congressional Research Service (December 1980), 2.

19. Leo Grebler, Joan W. Moore, and Ralph C. Guzman, *The Mexican American People: The Nation's Second-Largest Minority* (New York: The Free Press, 1970), 526.

20. Carey McWilliams, *North from Mexico: The Spanish-Speaking People of the United States* (New York: Greenwood Press, 1968), 102.

21. Julian Samora, Joe Bernal, and Albert Peña, *Gunpowder Justice: A Reassessment of the Texas Rangers* (Notre Dame, IN: Univ. of Notre Dame Press, 1979), 5.

22. T. R. Fehrenbach, cited in ibid., 12.

23. In ibid., 63.

24. Ibid., 1.

25. Paul S. Taylor, *Mexican Labor in the United States* (Berkeley and Los Angeles: Univ. of California Press, 1932), 8:27.

26. Ibid., 8:134.

27. In Gamio, *Mexican American Immigration to the United States*, 119.

28. Antonio M. Stevens Arroyo, "Puerto Rican Migration to the United States," in Sandoval, *Fronteras*, 274.

29. Carey McWilliams, *Ill Fares the Land: Migrants and Migratory Labor in the United States* (Boston: Little, Brown and Co., 1942), 158.

30. Armando Morales, *Ando Sangrando: A Study of Mexican American–Police Conflict* (La Puente, CA: Perspective Publications, 1974), 34;

National Commission on Law Observance and Enforcement, *Report on Crime and the Foreign Born* (United States Government, 1931), 230.

31. McWilliams, *North from Mexico*, 248.

32. Mary Gordon, "I Can't Stand Your Books: A Writer Goes Home," *New York Times Review of Books* (December 11,1988), 1.

33. Arthur J. Drossaerts, quoted in Rodolfo Acuña, *Occupied America: The Chicano's Struggle toward Liberation* (San Francisco: Canfield Press, 1972), 166.

34. Alberto Camarillo, "Mexican American and Non-Profit Organizations," paper presented at the Conference on Hispanics and the Independent Sector, University of San Francisco (November 14–16, 1988), 4.

35. McWilliams, *North from Mexico*, 189ff.

5. The Struggle for Rights

1. Juan Romero, "History of PADRES," paper presented at the CEHILA symposium in Las Cruces, New Mexico (January 15–17, 1988).

2. David Gómez, *Somos Chicanos: Strangers in Our Own Land* (Boston: Beacon Press, 1973), 9.

3. Paul Baca, "Preparation of Hispanic Priests for the United States," talk presented at the First National Encuentro, Washington, DC (June 19–22, 1972). Though Baca did not mention the name of the archbishop in his talk, he later told the author it was Vehr.

4. Moises Sandoval, *Our Legacy—The First 50 Years* (Washington, DC: League of United Latin American Citizens, 1979), 38.

5. James Dolan, "Ethnicity and Race," talk presented at the Newark hearing of the US Bishops' "Call to Action" (December 4–6, 1975).

6. Leo Grebler, Joan W. Moore, and and Ralph C. Guzman, *The Mexican American People: The Nation's Second-Largest Minority* (New York: The Free Press, 1970), 456.

7. Tony Castro, *Chicano Power—The Emergence of Mexican Americans* (New York: E. P. Dutton, 1974), 107.

8. Moises Sandoval, "Effects of World War II on the Hispanic People," in *Fronteras: A History of the Latin American Church in the USA since 1513*, ed. Moises Sandoval (San Antonio: Mexican American Cultural Center, 1983), 371.

9. Ibid.

10. Virgil Elizondo, quoted in ibid.

11. In Moises Sandoval, "The Church and El Movimiento," in Sandoval, *Fronteras*, 398.

12. Ibid., 399.

13. Gloria Gallardo, quoted in ibid., 406.

14. In Sandoval, "The Church and El Movimiento," 406.

15. Ibid., 406–7.

16. Ibid., 408, citing report by Las Hermanas.

17. Archbishop Francis J. Furey, interview with author.

18. Ibid.

19. Antonio M. Stevens Arroyo, *Prophets Denied Honor: An Anthology of the Hispanic Church in the United States* (Maryknoll, NY: Orbis Books, 1980), 176–77.

20. Report of the Citizens Advisory Panel to the Governor of New Mexico (September 1980), 2.

21. The remark that they "beat at our own game" is attributed to Father Vicente Lopez, a prominent member of PADRES, in Romero, "History of PADRES," 34.

22. Cardinal John Krol, quoted in Moises Sandoval, "Church Structures for the Hispanics," in Sandoval, *Fronteras*, 429.

23. Bishop Patricio Flores, "The Church: Diocesan and National," address to the First National Pastoral Encuentro, Washington, DC (June 19–22, 1972).

24. Archbishop Francis J. Furey, interview with author,

25. James V. Casey, "Church Concerned," *Denver Catholic Register* (March 29, 1973).

26. Frank Ponce, interview with author.

27. This is what officials of the USCC estimated the Third National Encuentro process cost, including the diocesan, regional, and national *encuentros*, plus the various meetings of the committees involved.

28. Martin McMurtrey, *Mariachi Bishop: The Life Story of Patrick Flores* (San Antonio: Corona Publishing Co., 1987), 51.

29. Moises Sandoval, "The Latinization Process," in Sandoval, *Fronteras*, 453.

30. Moises Sandoval, "Hispanic Challenges to the Church," paper prepared for the Secretariat for Hispanic Affairs, United States Catholic Conference (June 1978), 54.

6. Ministers and Ministry

1. Ken Johnson Mondragon, "The Educational Attainment of Hispanic Catholics in the U.S. and Its Impact on Pastoral Leadership in the Catholic Church," *¡En Marcha!* [Secretariat for Hispanic Affairs, United States Conference of Catholic Bishops] (Winter/Spring 2003), 13.

2. National Conference of Catholic Bishops, "Prophetic Voices: The Document on the III Encuentro Nacional de Pastoral" (1987).

3. Talk at Mexican American Cultural Center, 1992.

4. Leo Grebler, Joan W. Moore, and Ralph C. Guzman, *The Mexican American People: The Nation's Second-Largest Minority* (New York: The Free Press, 1970), 465.

5. Moises Sandoval, "Church Structures for the Hispanics," in *Fronteras: A History of the Latin American Church in the USA since 1513*, ed. Moises Sandoval (San Antonio: Mexican American Cultural Center, 1983), 415.

6. Ibid., 420.

7. Jay P. Dolan, *The American Catholic Experience: A History from Colonial Times to the Present* (New York: Doubleday, 1985), 375.

8. Sandoval, "Effects of World War II on the Hispanic People," in Sandoval, *Fronteras*, 368.

9. Ibid., 418.

10. Encarnación Armas, quoted in ibid., 450.

11. Moises Sandoval, "Hispanic Challenges to the Church," paper prepared for the Secretariat for Hispanic Affairs, United States Catholic Conference (June 1978), 54.

12. Ibid., 38.

13. Bishop Patricio Flores, quoted in Sandoval, "Effects of World War II on the Hispanic People," 402.

14. Sandoval, "The Church and El Movimiento," 383, citing Grebler et al., *The Mexican American People*, 465.

15. Bishop Humberto Medeiros, quoted in Sandoval, "The Church and El Movimiento," 383.

16. Sandoval, "The Church and El Movimiento," 380.

17. Ibid., 383.

18. Cesar Chavez, quoted in ibid.

19. Cesar Chavez, "On Money and Organizing," talk delivered in La Paz, California (October 4, 1971).

20. Sandoval, "The Church and El Movimiento," 386.

21. Father Eugene Boyle, in ibid., 387.

22. David E. Hayes Bautista and Gregory Rodríguez, *The Chicano Movement: More Nostalgia than Reality*, report, Alta California Research Center (September 17, 1995).

23. Bishop Patricio Flores, talk, COPS first annual convention, San Antonio, Texas (1974).

24. Interview with author, East Los Angeles, California, 1986.

7. The Church and Immigrants

1. Ron Cruz, *¡En Marcha!* [Secretariat for Hispanic Affairs, United States Conference of Catholic Bishops] (Fall/Winter 2005), 1.

2. *Puerto Ricans in the Continental United States: An Uncertain Future*, report, US Commission on Civil Rights (October 1976), 18.

3. Ibid.

4. Northeast Catholic Pastoral Center for Hispanics, *The Hispanic Community, the Church and the Northeast Center for Hispanics* (New York: Northeast Catholic Pastoral Center for Hispanics, 1982), 19.

5. US Department of Commerce, "The Hispanic Population in the United States: March 1986 and 1987 (Advance Report)," Bureau of the Census, in *Current Population Reports* (August 1987), cited in Fran Gillespie, "Hispanics in the U.S. Labor Force: A Briefing Presented to the U.S. Catholic Conference" (February 5, 1988).

6. Paul Sedillo, "Liberty and Justice for All," San Antonio "Call to Action," proceedings, 17.

7. Northeast Catholic Pastoral Center for Hispanics, *The Hispanic Community, the Church and the Northeast Center for Hispanics*, 5.

8. Juan Clark, *Why? The Cuban Exodus: Background, Evolution and Impact in USA* (Miami: Union of Cubans in Exile, 1977), 16.

9. Bryan O. Walsh, "The Spanish Impact Here: How the Archdiocese Is Meeting the Challenge," *The Voice* (July 18, 1975).

10. Bryan O. Walsh, "'The Church and the City: The Miami Experience," *New Catholic World* (early 1980s, exact date unknown).

11. Juan Clark, "Cuban Exodus Fact Sheet," undated.

12. Walsh, "The Spanish Impact Here."

13. Leo Grebler, Joan W. Moore, and Ralph C. Guzman, *The Mexican American People: The Nation's Second-Largest Minority* (New York: The Free Press, 1970), 519.

14. Wayne Cornelius, *Mexican Migration to the United States: Causes, Consequences and U.S. Responses*, Migration and Development Study Group, Center for Migration Studies (Cambridge: MIT, 1978), 4–5.

15. Wayne A. Cornelius, "Illegal Mexican Migration to the United States: Recent Research Findings, Policy Implications and Research Priorities," Center for International Studies (Cambridge: MIT, May 1977), 2–3.

16. Ibid., 4.

17. Allan Figueroa Deck, SJ, "A Christian Perspective on the Reality of Illegal Immigration," talk given to the Priests' Senate of the Diocese of San Diego (February 15, 1978), 11.

18. Roberto Martínez, interview with author, published in Moises Sandoval, "Borderline Christianity," *US Catholic* (June 2001), 12.

19. Because Puerto Ricans have been citizens since 1917, they are not technically immigrants, but their experience on the mainland has been the same as if they had been foreigners.

8. Hispanic American Protestantism

1. R. Douglas Brackenridge and Francisco O. García-Treto, *Iglesia Presbiteriana: A History of Presbyterians and Mexican Americans in the Southwest* (San Antonio: Trinity Univ. Press, 1974), 3.

2. Ibid., 6–7.

3. Melinda Rankin, *Twenty Years among the Mexicans—A Narrative of Missionary Labor* (Cincinnati: Chase and Hall, 1875).

4. Thomas Herwood, *History of New Mexico Spanish and English Missions of the Methodist Episcopal Church from 1850 to 1910*, 2 vols. (Albuquerque: El Abogado Press, 1908–10), 1:22.

5. Alfredo Nañez, *Historia de la Conferencia Rio Grande de la Iglesia Metodista Unida* (Dallas: Bridwell Library, Southern Methodist University, 1981), 44–47.

6. Brackenridge and García-Treto, *Iglesia Presbiteriana*, 26.

7. Justo L. González, *The Development of Christianity in the Latin Caribbean* (Grand Rapids, MI: Eerdmans, 1969), 91–95.

8. Elmer T. Clark, *The Latin Immigrant in the South* (Nashville, TN: The Cokesbury Press, 1924). Clark, a denominational executive of the Methodist Episcopal Church, South, "pressed an attitude held by many Anglos who intended well. 'Socially the Cuban immigrant is of a better class than the Mexican. . . . It is not to be thought, however, that these Cuban immigrants are of such a high type that they can immediately take their places in American social life. Such is far from the case. They come from the Catholic environment . . . and for the most part they are poor, ignorant and superstitious; it is not to be expected that immigrants from a land wherein more than half the people are illiterate would be of the highest type. These Cubans, almost as much as the Mexicans, need the social and religious ministry of the Protestant Church'" (51–52).

9. In Brackenridge and García-Treto, *Iglesia Presbiteriana*, 128. Cf. Vernon M. McCombs, *From over the Border* (New York: Council of Women for Home Missions and Missionary Education Movement, 1925), 83.

10. Ibid., 117.

11. José Moreno Fernandez, *Hispanic Methodism in the Southern California Arizona Conference* (Rel.D. dissertation, The School of Theology at Claremont, 1973), 85–86; Nañez, *Historia de la Conferencia Rio Grande de la Iglesia Metodista Unida*, 87–89.

12. Brackenridge and García-Treto, *Iglesia Presbiteriana*, 84.

13. Leo D. Nieto, "The Chicano Movement and the Churches in the United States," *Perkins Journal* 29 (Fall 1975), 27.

14. Ibid., 37.

15. Christian Lalive d'Epinay, *El Refugio de las Masas—Estudio Sociológico del Protestantismo Chileno* (Santiago: Editorial del Pacifico, S.A., 1968). Cf. Jean Pierre Bastian, *Breve Historia del Protestantismo en América Latina* (Mexico, D.F.: Casa Unida de Publicaciones, S.A., 1986), 164–67.

16. Lalive d'Epinay, *El Refugio de las Masas*, 96.

17. David Maldonado, "Chicano Protestantism: A Conceptual Perspective" (Arlington, TX, mimeographed paper, 1975), 12–13.

9. The Future Hispanic Church

1. "Census Bureau Projects Tripling of Hispanic and Asian Populations in 50 years," *¡En Marcha!* (Summer 2004).

2. Mireya Navarro, "Is Spanish the Measure of Hispanic?" *The New York Times* (June 8, 2003), citing a major national survey by the Hispanic Research Center, Washington, DC, and the Kaiser Family Foundation.

3. Ibid.

4. D. H. Lawrence, quoted in Carey McWilliams, *North from Mexico: The Spanish-Speaking People of the United States* (New York: Greenwood Press, 1968), 9.

5. David E. Hayes Bautista and Gregory Rodríguez, *The Chicano Movement: More Nostalgia than Reality*, report, Alta California Research Center (September 17, 1995).

6. Ben J. Wattenberg, "It Will Be a Smaller World after All," op-ed article, *The New York Times* (March 8, 2003).

7. Carlos Fuentes, *The Buried Mirror: Reflections on Spain and the New World* (New York: Houghton Mifflin Company, 1992), 348.

Bibliography

Acuña, Rodolfo. *Occupied America: A History of Chicanos*, 2nd ed. New York: Harper and Row, 1981.

Bañuelas, Arturo J., ed. *Mestizo Christianity: Theology from the Latino Perspective*. Maryknoll, NY: Orbis Books, 1999.

Chavez, Fray Angelico. *My Penitente Land: Reflections on Spanish New Mexico*. Albuquerque: Univ. of New Mexico Press, 1974.

———. *The Old Faith and Old Glory: The Story of the Church in New Mexico since the American Occupation (1846–1946)*. Santa Fe: Santa Fe Press, 1946.

Chicago Religious Task Force on Central America. *Dangerous Memories: Invasion and Resistance since 1492*. Chicago: Chicago Religious Task Force on Central America, 1991.

Clark, Juan. *Why? The Cuban Exodus: Background, Evolution and Impact in USA*. Miami: Union of Cubans in Exile, 1977.

De La Torre, Miguel A., and Edwin David Aponte. *Introducing Latino/a Theologies*, Maryknoll, NY: Orbis Books, 2001.

Deck, Allan Figueroa. *The Second Wave: Hispanic Ministry and the Evangelization of Cultures*. New York: Paulist Press, 1989.

———. *Frontiers of Hispanic Theology in the United States*. Maryknoll, NY: Orbis Books, 1992.

Diamond, Jared. *Guns, Germs, and Steel: The Fates of Human Societies*. New York: W. W. Norton, 1999.

Diaz-Stevens, Ana María. *Oxcart Catholicism on Fifth Avenue: The Impact of the Puerto Rican Migration upon the Archdiocese of New York*. Notre Dame, IN: Univ. of Notre Dame Press, 1993.

Dolan, Jay P. *The American Catholic Experience: A History from Colonial Times to the Present*. New York: Doubleday, 1985.

———. *The American Catholic Parish: A History from 1850 to the Present*. New York: Paulist Press, 1987.

———. *The Notre Dame History of Hispanic Catholics*. 3 vols. Notre Dame, IN: Univ. of Notre Dame Press, 1994.

Dunne, John Gregory. *Delano: The Story of the California Grape Strike*. New York: Farrar, Straus and Giroux, 1967.

Dussel, Enrique, ed. *The Church in Latin America 1492–1992*. Maryknoll, NY: Orbis Books, 1992.

———. *Historia General de la Iglesia en America Latina*. Vol. 1, *Introducción General*. Salamanca: Ediciones Sígueme, 1983.

Elizondo, Virgil P. *The Future Is Mestizo: Life Where Cultures Meet*. Oak Park, IL: Meyer-Stone Books, 1993.

Fuentes, Carlos. *The Buried Mirror: Reflections on Spain and the New World*. New York: Houghton Mifflin Co., 1992.

Gamio, Manuel. *Mexican American Immigration to the United States: A Study of Human Migration and Adjustment*. New York: Dover Publications, 1971.

García, Mario T. *Mexican Americans: Leadership, Ideology and Identity, 1930–1960*. New Haven, CT: Yale Univ. Press, 1989.

Goméz, David F. *Somos Chicanos, Strangers in Our Own Land*. Boston: Beacon Press, 1973.

González, Roberto O., and Michael La Velle. *The Hispanic Catholic in the United States: A Socio-Cultural and Religious Perspective*. New York: Northeast Pastoral Center for Hispanics, 1985.

Grebler, Leo, Joan W. Moore, and Ralph C. Guzman. The *Mexican American People: The Nation's Second-Largest Minority*. New York: The Free Press, 1970.

Guerrero, Andrés G. *A Chicano Theology*. Maryknoll, NY: Orbis Books, 1987.

Hennesey, James. *American Catholics: A History of the Roman Catholic Community in the United States*. New York: Oxford Univ. Press, 1981.

Heyck, Denis Lynn Daly, ed. *Barrios and Borderlands: Cultures of Latinos and Latinas in the United States*. New York: Routledge, 1994.

Holland, Clifton L. *The Religious Dimension in Hispanic Los Angeles: A Protestant Case Study*. South Pasadena, CA: William Carey Library, 1974.

Hurtado, Juan. *Social Distance between the Mexican American and the Church*. San Antonio: Mexican American Cultural Center, 1975.

Matovina, Timothy, ed. *Beyond Borders: Writings of Virgilio Elizondo and Friends*. Maryknoll, NY: Orbis Books, 2000.

Matovina, Timothy, and Gerald E. Poyo, eds. *¡Presente! U.S. Latino Catholics from Colonial Times to the Present*. Maryknoll, NY: Orbis Books, 2000.

McMurtrey, Martin. *Mariachi Bishop: The Life Story of Patrick Flores*. San Antonio: Corona Publishing Co., 1987.

Meier, Matt S., and Feliciano Rivera. *The Chicanos: A History of Mexican Americans*. New York: Hill and Wang, 1972.

Meléndez, Guillermo, ed. *Sentido Histórico del V Centenario, 1492–1992*. San José, Costa Rica: DEI, 1992.

Meyer, Jean A. *The Cristero Rebellion: The Mexican People between Church and State 1926–1929*. New York: Cambridge Univ. Press, 1976.

Mosqueda, Lawrence J. *Chicanos, Catholicism, and Political Ideology*. New York: Univ. Press of America, 1986.

Nevins, Albert J., MM. *American Martyrs from 1542*. Huntington, IN: Our Sunday Visitor, 1987.

Northeast Catholic Pastoral Center for Hispanics, *The Hispanic Community, the Church and the Northeast Center for Hispanics*, New York: Northeast Catholic Pastoral Center for Hispanics, 1982.

Perez, Arturo. *Popular Catholicism: A Hispanic Perspective*. Washington, DC: The Pastoral Press, 1988.

Pineda, Ana María, and Robert Schreiter, eds. *Dialogue Rejoined: Theology and Ministry in the United States Hispanic Reality*. Collegeville, MN: The Liturgical Press, 1995.

Puerto Ricans in the Continental United States: An Uncertain Future. Report. US Commission on Civil Rights. October 1976.

Pulido, Alberto Lopez. *The Sacred World of the Penitentes*. Washington, DC: The Smithsonian Institution Press, 2000.

Rodríguez, Jeanette. *Our Lady of Guadalupe: Faith and Empowerment among Mexican American Women*. Austin: Univ. of Texas Press, 1994.

Romero, C. Gilbert. *Hispanic Devotional Piety: Tracing the Biblical Roots*. Maryknoll, NY: Orbis Books, 1991.

Romero, Juan, and Moises Sandoval. *Reluctant Dawn: Historia del Padre A. J. Martínez, Cura de Taos*. San Antonio: The Mexican American Cultural Center, 1976.

Sandoval, Moises, ed. *Fronteras: A History of the Latin American Church in the USA since 1513*. San Antonio: The Mexican American Cultural Center, 1983.

Stevens Arroyo, Antonio M. *Prophets Denied Honor: An Anthology of the Hispanic Church in the United States*. Maryknoll, NY: Orbis Books, 1980.

Swadesh, Frances Leon. *Los Primeros Pobladores*. Notre Dame, IN: Univ. of Notre Dame Press, 1974.

Weber, David J. ed. *Foreigners in Their Native Land: Historical Roots of the Mexican Americans*. Albuquerque: Univ. of New Mexico Press, 1973.

Weigle, Marta. *The Penitentes of the Southwest*. Santa Fe: Ancient City Press, 1970.

Index